I0327264

# Fatal Mission

## The Life And Death Of The Crew Of Naughty Nan 467 SQN RAAF

Mal Elliott

16pt

# Copyright Page from the Original Book

Copyright © Mal Elliott

First published 2019

Copyright remains the property of the authors and apart from any fair dealing for the purposes of private study, research, criticism or review, as permitted under the Copyright Act, no part may be reproduced by any process without written permission.

All inquiries should be made to the publishers.

Big Sky Publishing Pty Ltd
PO Box 303, Newport, NSW 2106, Australia
Phone: 1300 364 611
Fax: (61 2) 9918 2396
Email: info@bigskypublishing.com.au
Web: www.bigskypublishing.com.au

Cover design and typesetting: Think Productions

Proudly printed and bound in China by Hang Tai Printing Company Limited

A catalogue record for this book is available from the National Library of Australia

For Cataloguing-in-Publication entry see National Library of Australia.

Creator: Mal Elliott
Title: Fatal Mission: The Life and Death of the Crew of Naughty Nan

# TABLE OF CONTENTS

*For Oscar, the crew of Naughty Nan, and the other 55,000 airmen to whom so much is owed by so many.*

*May they never be forgotten.*

423700 Flight Sergeant Oscar Skelton Furniss, RAAF 12 July 1921–4 May 1944

# ACKNOWLEDGEMENTS

This book is very much a personal history, compiled from family memories and from a wealth of other supplementary sources. The strongest thread of memory comes from conversations with Oscar's sole surviving sibling, his younger brother, Anthony, who was just nine when Oscar left for Canada in 1942. I am very grateful to Anthony for sharing these memories, some still painful despite the passing of so many years, but no less vivid for the elapse of time.

My description of Oscar's service history is the product of many visits to the National Archives of Australia with its comprehensive collection of records and the valuable assistance of the very helpful Archives staff. I am grateful for the generous access I was granted to the 467 Squadron records which helped immeasurably as I reconstructed Oscar's service life. Likewise, the diaries and reports of the two surviving aircrew, referred to as 'evaders', Stan Jolly and Bob Hunter (see Appendixes 2 and 3 for extracts from the accounts of both evaders), and the flying log books of three of the crew were generously made available to me by their relatives. From this hotchpotch collection emerged a richly detailed story of Oscar's life as a trainee and member of Bomber Command and of his final mission and I thank these wonderful people for helping me uncover that story.

Howard Heeley, Secretary and Museum Trustee of the Newark Air Museum, formerly known as RAF Winthorpe, where the crew trained in 1944, was particularly helpful and I am grateful for his valuable assistance. I appreciate the use of articles by the late David Collins and printed in *The Dispersal,* the quarterly magazine published by Newark Air Museum. Permission was granted by the museum in memory of David and I can think of no better way to honour his work.

I would like to express my thanks to the children of Stan Jolly for their generous permission to use 'My Airforce Experience', Stan's unpublished autobiography. Stan compiled his memoirs as oral history in 1988 and these were updated by his children after his passing.

My gratitude extends also to the family of Bob Hunter for granting me direct access to his diaries and the oral history he passed to them. I am particularly grateful to Bob's late wife, Barbara Hunter, who added important descriptions, comments and explanations to his diary extracts.

A very welcome addition to this book came in the form of anecdotes from the late Flight

Lieutenant Jack Colpus, DFC. Jack flew Lancaster JA901, PO-N ('Naughty Nan'), more often than any other pilot and the annotations in his flying log added depth to my understanding of the 'personality' of Naughty Nan and the challenges any crew faced. I am indebted to his family for supplying Jack's log and granting permission for its use.

Valuable assistance was also provided by Dr Peter Burness at the Australian War Memorial, Leslie Jubbs, Angela Elliott, Cameron Elliott, Judy Elliott, Helen Edmunds, Ian S. Warren, Dr Heather Fisher, Keith and Lorna Skellorn, the Llansamlet Historical Society, the RAAF Museum at Bulls Creek in Perth, Colin Weaver, Chris Dean of the RAF Waddington Heritage Centre, Lieutenant Colonel Paul Corden (Australian Army), and Andrew Panton of the Lincolnshire Aviation Heritage Centre, RAF East Kirkby, where World War II Lancaster NX611 (LE-H, nicknamed 'Just Jane') is being restored for possible future flight.

Mark Summers at RAF Lichfield, which now operates as a road freight hub, took time from his busy day despite the fact that I had arrived without prior notice. Mark kindly granted me access to the remaining RAF buildings, accompanying me on a personal guided tour and providing background information as we walked. I thank him for his generosity.

The books I used as background reading for this story have been included as a bibliography and I am grateful to all these authors for their excellent research which significantly broadened my knowledge of the work of Bomber Command. I have also used material from interviews with Jack Colpus included in the *Australians at War* series by the University of NSW. My thanks to the Australian War Memorial for permission to use Susan Green's interview with Flight Lieutenant Frank Dixon, a pilot with 467 Squadron.

I will also be eternally grateful to the survivors of the Mailly-le-Camp raid who I met at Mailly in 2012 and 2014 and who very generously shared their stories and memories with me. Likewise, I appreciate the contributions of the residents of the Aube region of France, which encompasses Mailly-le-Camp, who lived through the air raid of 3/4 May 1944 and kindly recounted their stories to me. These people still remember the early hours of Thursday 4 May 1944 and were willing to share their memories. I would like to make special mention of Madame Isabel Farcy who was not quite three years old and living in Mailly on the night of the raid. I was amazed at the clarity of her recollections given her tender years at the time.

I would like to particularly thank Group Captain Don Hiller, RAF (Retd), who I first met in Mailly in 2012 and who has been a constant source of encouragement, information and support ever since.

Finally I would like to thank Catherine McCullagh who has taken my draft, written as a database of facts, figures and anecdotes, and massaged it into a richly detailed manuscript that now tells the story of Oscar and his crewmates with passion and sensitivity.

# INTRODUCTION

This book tells the story of my uncle, Oscar Skelton Furniss, a young Australian whose love of aircraft and yearning for adventure took him to the other side of the world to serve with the Royal Australian Air Force (RAAF) as a member of Bomber Command in the dark days of World War II. While it is Oscar's story, it is a tale that is impossible to tell in isolation and the narrative inevitably moves beyond his personal story to encompass the experiences of his six fellow aircrew at Royal Air Force (RAF) Base Waddington. The men flew an Avro Lancaster III, JA901, PO-N, from 467 Squadron, RAAF, under the leadership of Flight Sergeant, later Pilot Officer Colin Dickson, who was promoted at the briefing prior to his final mission. It was a dangerous occupation and survival rates were predictably low. On the night that Oscar's luck ran out, at approximately 12.15am on 4 May 1944 during a night mission to France, the Lancaster was shot down having just completed a bombing run over the barracks adjacent to the town of Mailly-le-Camp. Their aircraft in flames, two of the crew managed to bale out, landing in occupied France and miraculously evading the Germans for four months before that part of

France was liberated and the men eventually reached London. Of my uncle Oscar and four other crew members, there was only the news that they had died with their aircraft.

Such was the family's grief at the loss of this vibrant young man that, over the next 70 or so years, his name was rarely spoken and he merged into the shadows, becoming more ghost than substance, his entire existence gradually undermined to the point that he might never have lived at all. As the years passed, this increasingly came to trouble me, particularly once I took a position at the Australian War Memorial and began to realise just how many stories lay behind the 103,000 names on the Roll of Honour. So much effort was made to ensure that these names and the men and women whose existence they defined were not forgotten that I began to be haunted by the fact that my own Uncle Oscar had been almost forgotten by the very people who were his family. Not only did Oscar never know his six nephews and two nieces, more importantly, *they* never knew *him*.

Having reached this realisation and decided that his story had to be told, I was finally spurred into action by the sober truth that the health of Oscar's last sibling, his younger brother Anthony, was slowly failing. If I did not capture his memories of the older brother he had idolised, they would die with him when finally he passed on. This was my last chance to ensure that Oscar lived again in the memory of his family and his growing list of descendants and that the spectral figure would emerge from the shadows to regain his humanity and become the real, tangible young man he once was.

So I set to my task, writing much of this story from a personal perspective, reconstructing Oscar's early life and recreating his experiences in Canada under the Empire Air Training Scheme. This was no easy task as his flying log has been lost to the family and that part of his story can never be told. Gradually, as I mapped Oscar's experiences, I realised that I needed to move beyond my focus on him alone and encompass the lives of the men who became his family during his wartime career—his crew. By the time I had concluded my research, even his aircraft, the Lancaster bomber known as 'Naughty Nan', had become a personality in the narrative, the object of the crew's unswerving affection despite the fact that she was generally regarded as a 'temperamental and unreliable kite' by the men themselves. Her fate, of course, is inseparable from those of the five crew members who perished with her in a field in France.

After a lengthy search and some amateur sleuthing, I managed to contact the families of five of the six other crew members, including the children of the two survivors and Stan Jolly's widow. These were emotional meetings and I experienced first-hand the suffering of the other families left behind. For some of these people their grief remains palpable even after 70 long years. Their memories of the young men they lost and who were Oscar's closest friends to the end were vital to this story, just as the story provided a crucial link to their boys. For them, my telling of this story has been of almost immeasurable importance.

As the story took shape, I began to realise that, while the people were central, there were places that also held extraordinary significance. With the realisation that many of the RAF stations where Oscar trained have all but disappeared, I embarked on a mission to visit and photograph these bases. These stations were home to the young men of Bomber Command and, as in the case of Oscar and four of his crew, the places where they spent their last days on this earth. They bore witness to the incredible triumph of the human spirit and, sometimes in equal measure, the deepest sadness.

This book is, above all, the story of a young man who, alongside 55,000 others, cherished a dream that ultimately cost him his life. That the dream he pursued with such fervour also saw him fight for his country and the cause of freedom in one of humanity's worst conflicts is probably no coincidence. As Oscar himself will reveal in the pages of this book, noble ambition was part of the idealistic dreams of young men of his age. Indeed this simply reinforces the fact that he, his crew and the thousands of others who fought in the skies across the breadth of western Europe do not deserve to be forgotten. In the pages of this book, Oscar will live and fly again and a new generation will discover the young man who perished over a field in France on his last, fatal mission.

Malcolm David Furniss Elliott
Canberra, 2019

# CHAPTER I

# THE BOY FROM WENTWORTH FALLS

Nurse Dayhew's 'Yenwood' Private Hospital, conveniently located directly across the road from the newly constructed Furniss home in Northumberland Road, Auburn, New South Wales, was an unprepossessing building with scrubbed floors and an air of starched efficiency on 12 July 1921, the day that Oscar Skelton Furniss made his appearance. Bertha Furniss was duly primped and preened and her new baby washed and swaddled, ready to greet her husband, ushered in by the bustling nurse. Bertha had already delivered a son, Frank, to her prosperous businessman husband, Oscar, but he was no less overjoyed by the arrival of a second son, whom he proudly named Oscar, as if to herald the onset of a dynastic line of Oscar Furnisses.

Two years later the Furniss family packed its goods and chattels and moved to the tiny, picturesque Blue Mountains village of Wentworth Falls. Oscar Furniss had spied that most precious of gems, a business opportunity. He had purchased Barr Real Estate, its offices occupying a prominent position at number 25 Station Street, opposite the railway station and next door to the Post Office.[1] Oscar Furniss was determined to make his mark as a purveyor of quality real estate and, as principal of the now renamed Barr & Furniss Real Estate, he also added Justice of the Peace to his growing list of credentials. A man with a sound business head, he was a firm believer in the importance of occupying the vital ground, and proximity to the railway line, the principal form of transport from the busy heart of Sydney, was utterly essential. He regarded the railway as simply a means of carriage for potential customers of the Sydney well-heeled variety. Given the fashion for escaping the unhealthy and unwholesome conditions of the city to take health treatments at such establishments as the Queen Victoria Sanatorium, which lay in the clean and restorative air of the mountains, he reasoned that these gentlefolk must, of course, be in need of a holiday house in charming Wentworth Falls. He was just the man to ensure that their needs were met.

# 3

The Furniss family home over the Barr & Furniss Real Estate office in Station Street, Wentworth Falls, circa late 1920s (Furniss family image).

For all that the Furniss family was among the better-known of the village's residents, Oscar was content to raise his family in the rambling apartment above the Furniss & Barr Real Estate office, reasoning that he would lose valuable time commuting from a separate house in the village. Bertha was likewise content, enjoying her view over the railway station which disgorged fashionably dressed visitors—the subject of some fascination—at regular intervals. Little Oscar would not be the last of Bertha's children and, in 1923, she gave birth to a daughter, Muriel. Ten years later, to her surprise, another son arrived whom the couple named Anthony and, four years on, a daughter Anne completed the brood. By then Bertha must have considered her duty well and truly done.

Bertha Furniss, c.1942 (Furniss family image).

The young Oscar grew up amid the natural beauty of Wentworth Falls where the scrubby, dappled eucalyptus forest gave way to sheer cliffs, rocky outcrops and dizzying overhangs, every crevice clad in a lush, tangled mantle of greenery.

Far below, the valley floor wove a carpet of thick green foliage which extended as far as the eye could see. The richly varied bush setting was a haven for the adventurous and the village youngsters claimed it as their own. Oscar attended Wentworth Falls Primary School, a three-room, three-teacher school which was considered large and extensive for a country school. The local children sat dutifully at their wooden desks copying verses and mathematics from the chalkboard and trying desperately to concentrate through the hot, dry summers and to keep warm in the icy winters, the school's playground often covered in a thick mantle of snow.

Having outgrown the tiny primary school, Oscar joined his brother Frank at Katoomba Intermediate High in 1934 where he embarked on his journey through secondary education. Oscar was a conscientious student with a healthy interest in learning, although he could be somewhat selective in his efforts. At the end of 1936 he dutifully stood before his father, watching as the elder Oscar Furniss brandished the letter containing his Intermediate Certificate results. The smug satisfaction on the young man's face deepened with his father's announcement that he had passed his maths subjects and, indeed, noted Furniss Pater with pride, he had scored a First Class pass in Maths II. His results in English, French, Latin and science were likewise the source of deep satisfaction and his father beamed approvingly. However the senior Furniss brow darkened with the move to his son's history results. Yes, the results were equally stellar, but quite the reverse. Oscar had failed dismally, sacrificing history to concentrate on his other subjects.

Oscar remained at Katoomba Intermediate High until April 1937, when he left school to accept the offer of work on a dairy farm at Kyogle on the north coast of New South Wales. He was aged just 15 years and nine months, but was following a common trend among those of his generation. Schooling was compulsory until the age of 14 and, beyond this point, most parents saw little benefit in keeping children at school when they could be earning a living to help support the family or making their own way in the world. University was a dream that was generally the province of the wealthy and was not among the plans entertained by Oscar Furniss for his sons. Bertha Furniss however, had her own ideas for her second son. She was tired of the pressures of real estate that seemed to take her husband away from home at every turn and longed for some stability. She cherished the hope that Oscar would eventually become a gentleman farmer, establishing a holding on the fertile flood plain of the Nepean-Hawkesbury River that flows north, below the eastern escarpment of the Blue Mountains, 50 kilometres west of Sydney. There she hoped to share his idyllic life among fruit orchards and dairy cattle on the rich alluvial soils of the river flats, the soft lowing of cows replacing the rattle of the steam engines that laboured up and down the mountains.

But the unfortunate Bertha was ripe for disappointment as the hard life of a dairy farmer would fail to snare Oscar's imagination despite the impossibly beautiful countryside in which he now lived. Lush pastures of electric green swept across hill and dale, bordered by verdant temperate rainforest. The pace of life was unhurried and generally dictated by the fat, contented cows which walked themselves to the dairy and stood obligingly as Oscar completed the milking rounds. But the hours were long and the chores endless and, after six months, Oscar moved on, seeking some variety. He was to experience more of the vicissitudes of farming over the next year, working initially on a sheep and wheat property surrounded by endless golden fields and cursed by the relentless need for rain. No happier here, Oscar moved again, finding employment in orchards close to home where he remained until the end of 1938. Perhaps it had been homesickness as much as the need for variety that had driven him from place to place.

In 1939 Oscar Furniss senior responded to his son's apparent affinity for the land and supported his enrolment at Hawkesbury Agricultural College, hoping the young man would at least learn the basics of farming technique and graduate with a qualification of some description. As a businessman, Furniss senior could see the value in a career on the land, but only if it followed a sound course of preparation and training.

Hawkesbury Agricultural College was a well-respected institution in 1939 and, now part of the University of Western Sydney, is still regarded as one of the foremost agricultural institutions in the country. Established in 1891, its opening sent a clear signal that agriculture was to play a major role in the economic prosperity of the colony of New South Wales and that of the nation itself. The college is situated in the tiny town of Richmond which nestles in soft, green countryside close to the escarpments that define the rise of the Blue Mountains, on the lush plains that bound the Nepean River. The town is sited some 65 kilometres north-west of Sydney on a feeder line from the suburban railway network that serves the city, then a mere two hours' travel by steam train. Oscar spent three years at Hawkesbury, studying horticulture and graduating in 1941 with a Diploma of Agriculture. Like the other students, Oscar boarded at the college. Despite this, Hawkesbury was close enough to home for him to feel the shadow of his father as he completed his studies, the memory of his stellar failure in history and the consequent wrath of Furniss Pater sufficient to ensure his dedication to his schooling—at least at first.

To Oscar's dismay, he soon discovered that returning to study would not guarantee him an escape from farmyard chores. One of the duties of the students at Hawkesbury was the daily milking of the college's cows. A number of Oscar's classmates had grown up on dairy farms and, having endured the lifelong chore of milking, they flatly refused to perform this duty at college. Consequently, given his six months' experience on a dairy farm, Oscar's daily routine now also featured the morning milking roster.

Despite the potential ire of his father, however, Oscar's report cards chart a decline in his initial enthusiasm for agriculture as the course progressed. Comments such as 'not displaying sufficient interest' and 'more diligence required' were not simply the result of muted protest over the milking roster. Something else was distracting Oscar and successfully diverting his attention from what were supposed to be studies that would equip him for his chosen career.

On the other side of the railway line from the college is the RAAF's Richmond Air Base. A number of the college's young men regularly gathered to watch entranced as aircraft such as the sleek, silver Hawker Demon and the much larger twin-engine Avro Anson were put through their paces. Several found their interest in farming now wavering as the metallic forms swooped and glided over the grounds of the college. Among these young men was one Oscar Furniss.

Oscar seated next to the College Principal, Mr E. Southee, for his senior year photo in 1941 (image courtesy of Hawkesbury Agricultural College).

The declaration of war in 1939 was to cause a steady leaching of agricultural students from Hawkesbury, all keen to turn their 'ploughshares to swords'. By the end of 1943, a total of 663 students had enlisted in the armed services with 177 opting to join the RAAF. Indeed, over the next two years, Oscar would meet a number of

Hawkesbury graduates at air bases in Australia, Canada and the United Kingdom (UK).

Oscar Furniss had long cherished an interest in aircraft and, alongside his brother Frank and Frank's best friend Gordon Hughes, had built model aircraft of every shape and size since he was a small boy. Frank had followed his own passion for aviation, studying by correspondence to obtain his wireless operator's licence in mid-1938 and then securing a position with Qantas Empire Airways. During World War II Frank would regularly fly the 'double sunrise' flight between Perth and Ceylon (modern Sri Lanka) as a member of the Qantas aircrew in a PBY Catalina in what remains the longest nonstop passenger service in aviation history at 32 hours' duration.

But Oscar was not interested in civil aviation, his senses mesmerised by the flash of forms that danced the skies above RAAF Base Richmond. He conceded that he would have to complete his Diploma of Agriculture, if for no other reason than to appease his long-suffering father who, after all, had financed his studies. But he was well aware that he would now use his diploma not to secure an agricultural plot on the banks of the Nepean River, but as collateral to enlist in the RAAF. Oscar wanted to fly.

By the time of his graduation from Hawkesbury at the end of 1941, Oscar was ready for his career change. A determined and headstrong young man, he was utterly adamant that he would be a pilot. He was a strapping lad, albeit not overly tall, standing just 5 feet 6 inches (168 centimetres) in his stockinged feet and weighing 9 stone 7 pounds (60 kilograms). Oscar was also a competent roadside mechanic, having dabbled in both motorbikes and cars, and a proficient sportsman at golf, tennis and table tennis. Like many country lads of his era, he was an excellent marksman and owned an FN .22 rifle.

In December 1941, Oscar Furniss finally made his life-changing decision. Certain that aviation rather than agriculture would satisfy his passion for adventure, Oscar presented himself at the Air Force Reserve Depot at Woolloomooloo and completed his application for entry to the Air Force Reserve. Like hundreds of other young hopefuls, desperately keen to serve their country in the RAAF, he now waited anxiously at home for the postman's whistle, eager for news that he had been accepted. Oscar realistically assessed his chances as mixed and now cast around for some means of improving his qualifications. He noted that one of the entry requirements for aspiring aircrew was proficiency in Morse Code. Postmasters and postmistresses the length and breadth of the country conducted after-hours courses in Morse Code for young hopefuls who sought entry to the Air Force Reserve. For Oscar, this meant a brief 10-metre walk across First Lane from his home to the Post Office. The standard course provided 21 lessons and Oscar had no doubt that he could master the complexities of Morse given sufficient time and tuition. He gave little thought to the grim alternative—a return to farming should the Air Force decide it had no need of the services of one Oscar Furniss.

Oscar home from college on his Matchless motorbike, June 1941 (Furniss family image).

# CHAPTER 2

# A PASSION FOR FLYING

The Air Force Reserve to which the hopeful Oscar Furniss applied in December 1941 was a combination of the Active Citizens Air Force (ACAF) and the RAAF Reserve. Established in 1925, four years after the formation of the RAAF itself, its core roles notably included the useful employment of the large pool of highly experienced and often decorated World War I airmen. During the Great War, these airmen had served in the Australian Flying Corps, then a unit of the Australian Imperial Force, flying in Europe and the Middle East and performing tasks such as reconnaissance, artillery spotting and bombing while also fighting their highly skilled adversary, the German Air Force.

In the 14 years between the formation of the ACAF and the outbreak of World War II, the ACAF squadrons were the mainstay of training within the RAAF. By September 1939 approximately two-thirds of those wearing an Air Force uniform were reservists. This ratio was consistent with the original expectations at the time of the RAAF's formation. At the outbreak of war, ACAF members were called up for the duration of the conflict and most transferred to the Permanent Air Force in order to serve overseas with Australian forces in Europe and the Middle East. This transfer was necessary because, under the *Defence Act 1903,* Army and Air Force reservists could not serve outside Australia's territorial borders. The ACAF squadrons operated more than 20 types of aircraft and made a considerable contribution to the overall operational efficiency of the RAAF.

By 1940 Australia's territorial borders included New Guinea and a large part of the Indian Ocean. While ACAF personnel were restricted to service in Australia, the expanded national borders saw them also sent to New Guinea and areas of the south-west Pacific. By 1940 the war had already encroached on Australian territory in the form of marauding German raiders.

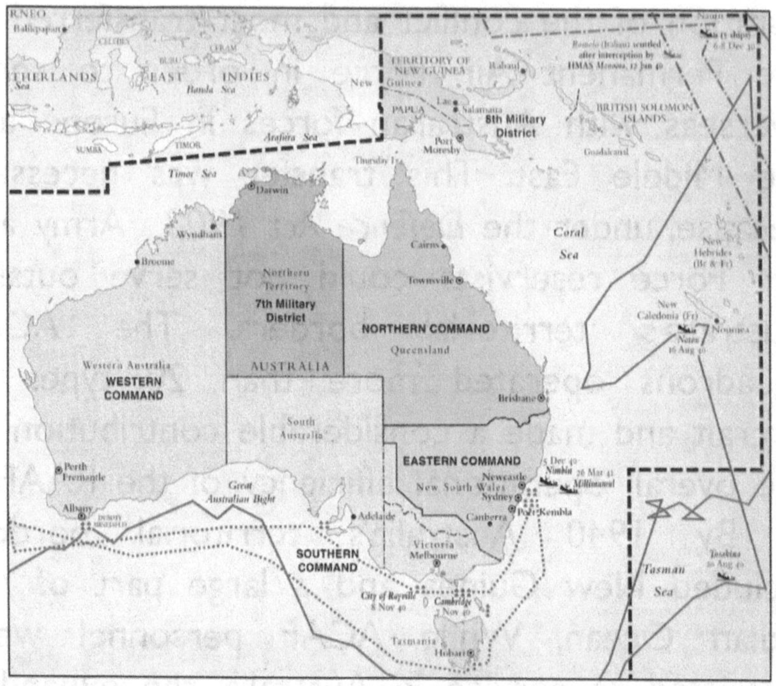


1940 map of Australia's territorial borders mark the tracks of German raiders off the Australian coastline (source: John Coates, Atlas of Australia's Wars, Oxford University Press, Melbourne, 2001).

Oscar Furniss celebrated his last Christmas with his family in December 1941. Soon after, he received a letter informing him that his application to join the ACAF had been successful and instructing him to proceed to No.2 Recruit Centre in Bradfield Park, Sydney (now the suburb of Lindfield), for recruit training. He farewelled his family in the early hours of 23 January 1942, his mother, Bertha, anxious and distressed that her time with her son was fast coming to an end. Oscar had become her favourite since Frank left home and she had taken some time to relinquish her dream of life on a dairy farm, cared for by Oscar and his family. This next phase of her life would simply have to wait until he returned when she would have more opportunity to persuade him to opt for the rural idyll she so desperately sought. She held Oscar close, releasing him only reluctantly for a final handshake with his father and a hug from his younger brother and sister. Oscar senior was increasingly proud of his second son, nurturing the image of a handsome young man in a deep blue uniform, pilot's wings adorning his breast. Yes, this was a profession that would see Oscar acquire some stability—the RAAF would make a man of him. As Oscar tripped down the stairs, past the office of Barr & Furniss Real Estate, crossing the street to take the train, as he had so many times before, he turned and waved, certain that his family—particularly his mother—would be watching. This time there would be no turning back. This time his journey would mark the start of the realisation of his dream to pursue his passion for flying.

Bradfield Park, on Sydney's north shore, had been planned as a garden suburb in memory of those involved in the design and construction of the Sydney Harbour Bridge.

In 1940 a RAAF base was established on the site and more than 200,000 RAAF and Women's Australian Auxiliary Air Force (WAAF) personnel were trained there during the heady days of World War II.

Like Oscar, the young Stan Jolly also cherished an ambition to fly. With the outbreak of World War II in 1939, the 17-year-old Stan had pondered the fact that, as some of his uncles had fought in World War I, it was probably his turn to fight in this latest war. However he was in no hurry to enlist at that point, preferring to bide his time and savour the delights of teenage life a little longer. The Air Force enjoyed limited publicity until the deadly duels fought in the Battle of Britain became the stuff of heroic news stories, inspiring the young Stan and spurring him to seek a career as a pilot. He was pleased to note that the Air Force uniform was far smarter than the drab khaki of the Army, delighted also to discover that pilots were not required to sleep in tents. But his burgeoning ambition brought Stan to a point of frank self-examination and he admitted somewhat sheepishly that his school results were mediocre at best and certainly lacked the brilliance he imagined was required of a fighter pilot. Deciding to invest in his future, Stan enrolled in evening classes with a teacher who lived nearby. However he had just met a beautiful young woman named Phyllis, for whom he was rapidly developing a deep affection, and any thought of enlistment had been delayed indefinitely. Fate was to intervene and, with the swift movement south of the Japanese in late 1941 and early 1942, the war began to encroach and Stan decided he could delay no longer, applying to join the Air Force in 1942. A series of interviews saw his name placed on the reserve list and he was sent home to await a call. Like Oscar, Stan completed a Morse Code and aircraft recognition course prior to his enlistment.

At the same time another young man named Jack Colpus, later to pilot the same Lancaster bomber in which Oscar flew his final missions, joined the RAAF Reserve in his home town of Perth, Western Australia. Jack had been a member of the militia 13th Field Ambulance for some years prior to the war but decided to join the RAAF after a friend was taken prisoner during the battle for Crete in mid-1941. Jack noted at the time that 'the air force seemed to be a better way of doing something, so I applied.' However, having set his sights on becoming a pilot, Jack realised that he needed a few extra qualifications:

> Before I actually went into camp and signed up, I was on the reserve for about

three or four months and I used to go into the GPO [General Post Office] and learn Morse and into Perth Tech [Technical College] ... to learn navigation and maths. So that was about two or three nights a week and that ultimately helped me a lot when I started training. When I was called up in September '41 I went into ANA House and had a medical and an IQ test and for some unknown reason the doctor said, 'You are only fit for a pilot because of your eyesight.' And I said, 'Well that's all right. Thanks.' So from there we signed up, made our declaration for King and Country and all the rest of it and went over to Pearce ... it was an excellent idea as far as I was concerned because when we got to Pearce I'd already brought myself up to the required standard for Morse so I didn't have to worry about that subject at all. I could concentrate on the other subjects which were navigation and the theory of flying and mathematics so that was really good. Helped me a lot.[2]

The first three days of Oscar's Air Force career saw him complete a lengthy series of medical and aptitude tests. No.2 Recruit Centre performed the essential task of training raw recruits from across the country and from all areas of society to bathe, shave, shine boots, polish buttons, maintain their uniforms and behave in the manner expected of them as members of the RAAF. Recruits came from a variety of backgrounds, many learning some of life's lessons for the first time. The recruit instructors, primarily corporals and sergeants, were keen to ensure that their charges quickly learned to maintain both the barracks and their kit in a fastidious and orderly manner. A significant amount of marching and drill was also part of the first six weeks' training, regarded by the instructors as 'character building'. Developing a sense of teamwork and a military ethos was likewise integral to service life. Developing bonds and strengthening mateship were crucial in managing the emotional upheaval of leaving home for these young men, some of whom had never travelled beyond the borders of their home state.

Jack Colpus described his recruit training at Pearce as dominated by drill sergeants who imposed a strict regime on the recruits:

> Well you ... get all your equipment of course and one of the other things that you do other than the ground subjects was square bashing [drill]. You know they had a couple of woolly sergeants there that tore the strips off you and got you down on the parade ground with your rifle and called

> you all the imaginable things under the sun. Stupid this etc. And so they smartened us up that way and the rest of the time was more or less studying and at the end of that you had an examination and that took a few months and then went on to Cunderdin ... [There] we had timber framed huts and they were pretty rough in as much as the bedding was what we used to call 'pig troughs'. They were just three boards, one flat and one each side on an angle held in a little trestle each end and the mattress was a palliasse it was just made out of bagging type material and one of your first jobs was to fill your palliasse with straw. It was a bed, but not the best. Not the most comfortable, but anyway we were all in the dormitory style place there and you had to fold your blankets in such a way and ... discipline ... The first thing you learn I think when you get into any service is ... to be disciplined, but fortunately I'd been disciplined well and truly at home so it was easy for me.[3]

Once Oscar had completed his six months of basic training, he was finally eligible for entry to the RAAF, with the strong probability that he would be sent overseas. On 18 July 1942, he officially enlisted 'for the duration of the war plus 12 months', the additional 12 months to cover a period of demobilisation at the end of hostilities which might see him repatriated over considerable distances. This additional period also covered care for those who had been wounded and required significant medical treatment. Australia's armed forces had learned a great deal from the enormous demobilisation effort at the end of the last war which had seen some men take a full 12 months to be repatriated.

Oscar's next period of instruction would now be conducted under the Empire Air Training Scheme, established in December 1939 in response to the outbreak of war with Germany. The scheme's ultimate aim was to supply the thousands of aircrew Britain would require for the looming air war over Europe. Structurally, the scheme was designed to ensure common training across the British Empire with elementary flying schools established in Australia and Canada and advanced schools in Canada and Rhodesia (modern Zimbabwe), an enticing prospect for those who had never travelled overseas. Graduates were then posted to operational squadrons—either Royal Air Force (RAF) or RAAF—in the UK.

The scheme's Australian schools trained young men up to aircrew standard, with courses for pilots and observers (later termed 'navigators' under a change in terminology effected in March 1942) lasting two years, while those for wireless operators and air gunners were just one year in duration. The rapid development in wartime radio and wireless technology soon saw the training of wireless operators extended to two years in duration. Some navigators were given additional training so that, should the circumstances require, they could fly the aircraft to some degree, holding it straight and level to assist the pilot, particularly in an emergency. Trainee pilots initially flew Tiger Moth biplane trainers which, after a number of close shaves, were uniformly painted bright yellow to increase their visibility. Having completed their initial hours, the trainee pilots were then upgraded to the single-engine Harvard trainers or the twin-engine Avro Anson that had so mesmerised Oscar Furniss during his Hawkesbury days.

Oscar on his enlistment day, 18 July 1942 (RAAF image).

Jack Colpus completed basic navigation and ground training over a period of three months at RAAF Base Pearce in Western Australia. He then moved to Cunderdin for basic flying training on Tiger Moths for another three months:

> [I]t was pretty intensive training ... about three months at Pearce, about three months at Cunderdin and then another three months at Geraldton ... it went through from September to July of the next year '42 ... at Pearce I had my 21st birthday ... [At] Cunderdin we did ground subjects but started flying the Tiger Moth and as it was getting hot they had problems with the planes landing during the hot part of the day so they started very early in the morning. We used to get up and get away about six o'clock in the morning and fly till about ten o'clock and then have a break in between, there'd be some ground subjects and then [we would] fly later in the afternoon. So there were four pupils to this particular instructor that I had and he wasn't a particularly happy sort of fellow and he scrubbed two of them pretty well straight away and that meant that there were just the two of us and we managed to get through but changed to another instructor about halfway through. This fellow ... used to abuse us a lot and ... swear and also he had a nasty habit of, if you didn't do the manoeuvre correctly you had a

joystick in front of you and he had a joystick in front of him and he used to get the joystick and whack it across to one side so it'd come across and whack you on the knee.

I had another unfortunate experience with him when we were doing a cross-country flight. We were down at Northam and he cut off the engine and he said, 'Right—now you do an emergency landing.' So there was the little Northam recreation ground down there and I headed down towards it and I didn't do a very good job. There were trees there and I didn't want to get close to them and anyway I didn't get down so he took over and said, 'This is how you do it.' So he went up and did it and landed and said, 'Right-o, get out.' So I got out and we had what was called a seat type parachute on in those days—the parachutes attached to a harness and the backside—and he said, 'Right get out here and walk down to that field there and just see how much was left when I did it.' So I walked down and back again and when I got back in he said, 'Right, and your weekend leave's cancelled.' [I was] not too happy.

> [O]ne night an alarm went off and we were woken up and a terrific storm came up and the Tiger Moths were all spread around the airfield and the wind was buffeting them up—they were anchored down with big concrete blocks but if they kept on doing that they'd eventually do damage—pull the wings off or something so we all went out and a couple of us laid over the wings and another down on the plane to hold them down so that was quite an experience ... That'd be a great photograph. A whole lot of flyers sprawled over their planes.[4]

On 19 July 1942, Oscar was officially posted to No.30 Aircrew Course at No.2 Initial Training School at Bradfield Park. His rank on enlistment was aircraftman volunteer and he was then remustered (the RAAF term for reclassification) to aircraftman second class. All aircrew commenced their training at this rank, at the very bottom of the RAAF's rank scale.

At this point in his RAAF career, Oscar and his fellow students had yet to be allocated a specific mustering (the RAAF term for a job specialisation). Unlike the Australian system of selection, the RAF's Bomber Command provided specific guidance on the influence of a young man's social background in determining his mustering, particularly his suitability for aircrew:

> Pilots, navigators and bomb aimers took two years to train and tended to be drawn from the university and grammar school element of aircrew intakes. Everyone wanted to be a pilot and those who failed the aptitude and preliminary flying tests were remustered as navigators and bomb aimers. Air gunners, flight engineers and wireless operators were trained in about nine months.[5]

The contrast between the social background of the English and Australian aircrews must have been starkly evident to RAF squadron leaders and wing commanders who received their Empire Air Training Scheme graduates at bases around the UK, perhaps often with a degree of surprise.

Initial instruction covered the basics of life in the Air Force, supplementing the training completed at No.2 Recruit Centre. Specific subjects included mathematics, navigation and aerodynamics. At the completion of the first eight weeks of the course, students were paraded before an Aircrew Categorisation Board consisting of five senior officers who sat at a large table covered with copies of a student's class work, exam results and reports. Based on this information, the board would determine where the student would fit best in the Air Force structure: pilot, navigator, wireless operator, air gunner or bomb aimer. While the board members would ask each candidate a series of questions, it was clear to most that the decisions had already been made.

Despite the fact that applicants were given the freedom to nominate for a particular mustering, their final career path was determined by factors beyond their control. Often it was attributes demonstrated during their initial flying training that would dictate their future mustering. For example, fighter pilots were drawn from those with quick responses and a natural aggression while navigators were required to possess a demonstrated strength in mathematics. Logically, the number of positions available for pilots was restricted and the best of each intake were slotted into those positions. Most applicants were eager to become pilots and Oscar was no different.

The first news Oscar received of his RAAF mustering arrived in the form of long lists pinned to the board the day after his interview, 10 September 1942. He joined the hopeful throng that gathered to read the lists, the trainees variously whooping with glee or standing back in muted disappointment to silently ponder the decisions that lay behind the neatly typed list.

Oscar struggled to reach the front of the crowd, eager to search for his name. He ran his finger down the list to discover that he had been allocated as 'Aircrew V (O)'—he would train as a navigator. Oscar nursed his disappointment, finally dispelling it with the conviction that, while he might never be a pilot, he would nonetheless be a crucial member of a closely knit team—and he would fly on operations. He would play his part in this war, albeit following a different path to the one he had originally marked for himself so many years ago.

When Stan Jolly was interviewed by the Air Categorisation Board he surprised the panel by announcing that he wanted to be a navigator, although he had clearly been working hard to earn selection as a pilot. When quizzed on his choice Stan made the very astute observation that, not only was navigation a fascinating pursuit, but ultimately, 'pilots had to go where a navigator told them'. Stan's first flights in an Avro Anson convinced him that he had made the right choice: an Avro Anson had a manual undercarriage and one of the tasks of the co-pilot was to wind it up and down.[6]

Another four weeks of instruction followed, the emphasis now on the mustering determined by the board. Oscar's career path to navigator was clearly influenced by his strength in Maths

II in his Intermediate Certificate. Stan Jolly was one of a group of navigators posted to Parkes to learn astro-navigation while Oscar completed his astro-navigation studies in Canada. Oscar and Stan were to meet nine months later in Wales and become crew mates shortly after. With a surplus of navigators in England in 1943, Stan changed career path to bomb aimer. That decision was to save his life.

Oscar completed his course at No.2 Initial Training School on 8 October 1942. Two days later he was promoted to leading aircraftman 2 (observer), the equivalent of an Army lance corporal and was informed that he would be completing his final navigator qualification training in Canada. Having never travelled further afield than northern and western New South Wales, Oscar was predictably elated. It was now certain that, once he completed his studies in Canada, he would be posted to Bomber Command in the UK. He would not pass the war on a dairy farm, watching enviously as his peers manoeuvred elegant fighters and sturdy bombers in the skies above. He would make his mark as a member of a front-line unit in a major conflict.

The last photo of Oscar at the family home in Wentworth Falls, mid-October 1942 (Furniss family image).

A posting to No.2 Embarkation Depot, also located at Bradfield Park, followed as he began his preparations for movement to Melbourne prior to embarkation for Canada. He spent his final few days of leave at home in Wentworth

Falls, drinking in the familiar surroundings and conscious that it would be some time—possibly years—before he would return. No-one could tell for certain how long this war would last. His father talked endlessly of possibilities for his son, both wartime and post-war, and Oscar revelled in his father's obvious pride. He knew he had not always enjoyed the unblemished favour of Furniss senior and was delighted to see how much joy his father took in his new career, terms such as 'noble' and 'patriotic' used with flourish to describe his calling, the older man clearly proud that his son was doing his duty in time of war. Bertha's response was far more muted. Yes, she was proud of her son, but she could not escape the sense of foreboding that this might be the last time she saw her boy, held him close, heard his cheery laugh. Oscar had consolidated his position as her favourite, his restlessness entrancing her, his vibrancy and quirkiness never failing to raise her spirits. He was so different to the dependable Frank, a free spirit who remained restive and transient until he had found what he regarded as his destiny. She farewelled him once more, this time with a deep sadness, fighting back the tears and desperate to believe that, one day, he would walk through the doors of 25 Station Street again.

On 31 October 1942 Oscar departed Bradfield Park for No.1 Embarkation Depot at Ascot Vale Showground in Melbourne. He boarded the train in Sydney, his smart, deep blue RAAF uniform complete with jaunty forage cap attracting the attention of several local lasses who lined the station to farewell a group of departing troops. Oscar was pleased to see that, amid the sea of khaki and olive green, the ocean blue of his uniform stood out—Jack Colpus remembered the RAAF as nicknamed 'the blue orchids'. Oscar smiled at the young women who giggled shyly back, and winked and waved at them from the window of the train, eliciting further giggles. This was one benefit of service life that he had yet to appreciate. The train moved off, puffing slowly from the platform at Central Station, and Oscar basked in his final moments of admiration before the engine gradually gathered pace, leaving the young women staring longingly, eventually swallowed by the clouds of steam that drifted across the platform. Oscar settled back to doze as the Sydney suburbs crawled by. Hours later, he woke at the railway station in the town of Albury where all passengers were forced to change trains. The unifying influence of Federation four decades earlier had left the railway system steadfastly unmoved and the railway gauges in every state remained obstinately different to their fellows, each state arguing that its gauge should become the national standard. Stalemate ensued and continued, forcing Oscar and his fellow travellers to change from the New South Wales trains that ran on a 4 foot 8 1/2 inch gauge to Victorian trains that travelled on the larger 5 foot 3 inch gauge. Jack Colpus, travelling to Melbourne from Perth, also found the difference in railway gauges disruptive:

> [The train to Melbourne was] pretty rough and ready [particularly] on the Nullarbor. We had to change at Kalgoorlie because in those days they didn't have standard gauge all the way and the train from Kalgoorlie across the Nullarbor used to stop in the middle of the desert there and [we would] get out and walk down the back and they'd have a cook house down the back and you'd have your meal and then get back on but it was minimal accommodation you know—it was just rough and ready.[7]

Several hours passed before Oscar stirred again, this time to catch his first glimpse of the outer suburbs of Melbourne as the train slowed on its final approach to Spencer Street Station. The young RAAF trainees disembarked and were herded unceremoniously into trucks for the drive to the tent city at the Ascot Vale Showground.

Life in the tent city was primitive and Oscar was glad that his stay would be mercifully short. He slept on a straw palliasse in a tent with five other trainees and queued to use the ablution block in the morning. He queued again for a breakfast of rather dubious quality and had just finished packing his kitbag when word arrived that the truck had returned to take the RAAF trainees to the docks at Port Melbourne. He bid a none too fond farewell to the tent city and swung himself onto the back of the truck to join his comrades. A pleasant drive through the city took them to the docks where they were assailed by a biting wind and the stench of rotting seaweed. Oscar began to hope fervently that his Canadian base would be located some distance inland.

Having left Australia, Oscar Furniss, like his fellow trainees, was transferred to the Royal Canadian Air Force for the duration of his training. In Oscar's case this lasted from 2 November 1942 until 25 May 1943. This was routine procedure under the agreement that governed the Empire Air Training Scheme—Oscar would be just one of almost 10,000 RAAF airmen trained by the Canadians during World War II. Many, among them the two men who would be members of Oscar's final aircrew, Stan Jolly and Bob Hunter, completed similar training in

Australia and then travelled via North America to the UK to finish their training. Each took a different route to the UK, Stan sailing from his home town of Brisbane direct to San Francisco, while Bob sailed from Sydney to San Francisco with a stopover in Auckland, New Zealand. From San Francisco, Stan and Bob took different rail routes across the United States (US) to New York and both sailed to the UK on the *Queen Elizabeth,* at different times and without completing aircrew training in North America. Others sailed to San Francisco and then travelled by train north to Canada or east to training facilities in the US.

Oscar's last glimpse of the Australian coastline as it disappeared beyond the horizon must have marked a bitter-sweet moment for him. He had left behind everything that had defined his life thus far: family, friends, home, college, his Matchless motorbike and the Australian bush that he loved so dearly. Like the young men around him, he longed to be part of the great adventure that was war. He was eager to test himself in the theatre of air combat and to become a member of a team that would take the air war to the German foe in the skies above occupied Europe. As Oscar watched the white-capped deep blue of the ocean race past, he must have wondered at the rapidity with which his dream to master the air was taking shape. And he must have pondered precisely what destiny had in store for him.

# CHAPTER 3

# FREEZING IN CANADA

If Oscar Furniss was nervous about his passage across the Pacific Ocean on his way to Canada, he showed no sign in his letters to his family. However, he certainly had cause for concern. Over the previous 12 months, Japan had entered the war with the bombing of the US base at Pearl Harbor on the Pacific island of Hawaii, while Darwin, Townsville and a number of other Australian centres had been bombed multiple times. Japanese submarines had also been active off the east coast, attacking shipping and inflicting substantial losses both in lives and vessels. Japanese forces now occupied a significant swathe of territory in the Pacific, and Australian and US soldiers had been involved in fierce fighting to Australia's immediate north. It was a dangerous time to be at sea and rigorous drills became a daily duty, a necessary precaution given the substantial risks to shipping posed by the ever-present Japanese submarines.

Oscar's first few days were marred by seasickness and he slept in a bare, cheerless cabin which he shared with several of his fellow trainees. Jack Colpus sailed from Perth direct to

England on the *Western Land* and also suffered from seasickness which he described as 'terrible':

> We were in a really long convoy and the worst part of it was that right at the back there was a very, very slow ship and it was obviously burning coal and it was pushing out some smoke and it was going very, very slowly. Well, the rest of the convoy had to go at the speed of the slowest ship so we headed off ... and I was five days on the back being seasick and feeling horrible and couldn't care if the ship went down. [There was] a fair amount [of seasickness on board] but I seemed to be one of the worst and fellows used to come down and say, 'What would you like to eat?' I said, 'A dry bun thanks.' A dry bun. That and some water, oh it was terrible.[8]

The threat of submarines remained uppermost in the minds of Oscar and his fellow passengers, the shadowing naval ship providing token comfort at best. When she departed in the waters off American Samoa, the abandoned passenger liners could only hope that the war had not spread to the north-eastern Pacific just yet.

But Oscar's luck held and the RAAF trainees breathed a collective sigh of relief when their ship finally sailed safely into San Francisco Bay to be greeted by the vastness that is the United States. San Francisco, as a harbour city, radiated similar charm to Sydney, its Golden Gate Bridge providing a welcome sight as the ship sailed regally beneath, on her way to her berth in the bay. The young Australians had little time to drink in the vista of the harbour and the city's impressive collection of skyscrapers as they were hurried to the ferries that would take them to shore. Once ashore, they would march through the city to the Vancouver train. The relaxed overnight train trip from Sydney to Melbourne was to prove a far cry from the berth that greeted them at San Francisco Station. They were to journey to Canada aboard a sealed troop train. As a leading aircraftman 2 (O), Oscar was not yet entitled to enjoy the privileges of rank and was forced to endure the 36-hour trip in spartan surroundings. However, dining in the relative smoothness of a railway dining car made a pleasant change after three weeks on the high seas. The trainees finally disembarked in Vancouver, Canada, on 27 November 1942, their 25-day journey from Australia over. At this point they were still unsure of their final destination, although rumour decreed that it would be either Malton, near Toronto, or Edmonton.

The Royal Canadian Air Force now became responsible for Oscar's health, wellbeing and training and he and his fellow trainees were immediately despatched to No.3 Manning Depot at Blatchford Field in Edmonton, Alberta. Edmonton lies around 1200 kilometres from Vancouver, a distance that took the Australians two days to traverse by train, their journey taking them through the spectacular Rocky Mountains. The men were once again accommodated in troop trains and, now accustomed to the cheerless carriages, took the opportunity to relax and enjoy the breathtaking scenery, aware that the hard work was soon to begin.

The staff of No.3 Manning Depot were well aware that the young Australians were now far from home—some for the first time in their short lives—and had organised a series of measures to assist the trainees to settle in. One such measure saw local families open their homes to the new arrivals who were invited for a family meal on a regular basis. Oscar and his friend Walter Weekes, from Harbord in Sydney, enjoyed the hospitality of the Watson family who were keen to ensure that the young Australians enjoyed all the comforts of home.

Walter Weekes with Mr and Mrs Watson, home hosts for trainee airmen in Edmonton, December 1942 (Oscar Furniss image).

Like the manning depots in Australia, No.3 conducted a number of courses for both ground and aircrew. Oscar attended No.2 Air Observers' School for a period of four weeks before taking a circuitous route south to Royal Canadian Air Base Pearce to join No.3 Air Observers' School for 16 weeks which would see him complete the 20-week course. These 20 weeks involved 900 hours of tuition of which 700 hours were spent in the classroom, and the trainees were under pressure to perform well from the outset. Topping the course meant an immediate commission while failure resulted in one of three much-dreaded options: 'back squadding', remustering or being sent home. Oscar realised that this was a course in which he had no choice but to excel—the consequences of failure were simply too awful to contemplate.

Stan Jolly's six-day crossing of the US was as far removed as possible from Oscar's spartan troop train. Stan travelled in style in a Pullman carriage with its own porter who made the beds, refreshing the linen a least once during the transcontinental trip. This was also Stan's introduction to the disposable era, the men's meals served on synthetic plates and the tables cleared by the porter who simply tossed the used plates in a bin. Stan's destination was Camp Miles Standish which provided yet another surprise for Stan—a Coca Cola vending machine stood solidly outside each accommodation hut. Stan was instructed to insert a nickel (five cents) into the slot, a rumble would follow and, to his delight, out popped an icy cold bottle of the dark, sugary liquid.

Bob Hunter sailed from Sydney on the USS *Mount Vernon* and was less than impressed with his cramped and unventilated four-man cabin. The trainees had flying fish for company on the way to Auckland and then a pod of whales as they headed north. The whales maintained the ship's speed of 20 knots for several hours and Bob was impressed. Less impressive was the heat as they neared the equator, prompting Bob and his mate Aubrey Thomas (known to all as 'Aub') to sleep on deck for most of the extremely hot nights. Like most other visitors, Bob was overwhelmed by the beautiful, sophisticated city of San Francisco, although he quickly adapted to the comforts of life in a Pullman car on the troop train across the US.

Oscar's new home at Air Base Pearce was an island of buildings in a vast expanse of flat, furrowed fields and reminded him of his time on a wheat farm in the arid emptiness of western New South Wales. His 20 weeks with the Royal Canadian Air Force was divided into eight weeks at Bombing and Gunnery School and 12 weeks at Air Observers' School.

During the first years of World War II, bombing over Europe had been highly inaccurate and characterised by frustratingly widespread imprecision. On many heavy bombers, the navigator doubled as the bomb aimer, and these men were soon being dangerously overworked. As a consequence, large numbers of bombs were being dropped miles from their target, while the crews flew off, blissfully unaware that they had missed their mark completely. When Air Marshal Arthur 'Bomber' Harris became Commander-in-Chief of Bomber Command in 1942 he sought to resolve this problem, initially adding a new crew member to most bombers. He called this additional crewman an 'air bomber'. As Harris explained:

> There was an obvious need to introduce the air bomber.... The navigator had more than enough to do ... to get the aircraft within a few miles of the target, especially when making the run up.... Apart from all the other difficulties ... the work he had done as a navigator left him no time to get his eyes conditioned to the darkness, which he would have to do before trying to spot the aiming point.[9]

This change to the composition of aircrew in bombers resulted in a restructure and expansion of air observer training in Canada. No.2 Air Observers' School was where the serious training of aircrew commenced and where Oscar completed hours of practice using the British P10 magnetic compass, the primary tool of his trade.

The use of the magnetic compass, sextant, drift recorder and various calculators added to the basic navigation skills of dead reckoning, visual landmark recognition and interpretation of aerial photography. The Avro Anson V twin-engine multi-purpose aircraft used for navigation training were modified to provide facilities for two navigators and sometimes a third student was squeezed into a spare seat.

The P10 magnetic compass and other navigation tools including watch, trip log, pencil, Douglas protractor to the left of the compass and the Dalton Navigation Computer above the compass (J.S. Bond image).

The difficulties inherent in flying by visual landmarks in Canada represented an entirely new challenge compared to Australia and to what the trainees would eventually experience in Europe. Outside the scattered main cities in Australia there were some sealed roads, railway lines and broad expanses of flat, dry farmland. In Canada the cities were quite different in composition, while the topography was far more varied and comprised multiple series of hills, huge mountain ranges and large bodies of water. Fortunately for novice navigators, every town had a grain silo with the local name painted on the side in very large letters. The fencing also followed the cardinal directions of north to south or east to west and the realisation that the sun was always in the south assisted orientation in the air. Complicating the issue further was the approach of what would be one of Canada's severest winters, with-50°F (-45.5°C) recorded in some centres. The luckless trainee navigators soon realised that topographical features tend to disappear under a blanket of snow.

Oscar wasted no time finding company in frozen Canada, pictured here with Gladys Shoen and Dot Mitchell in Edmonton, Christmas 1942 (Furniss family image).

At the Air Observers' School, Oscar also trained in bomb aiming and gunnery. The curriculum further included a smattering of non-navigational subjects including meteorology, aircraft recognition, current affairs, physical training and Morse Code. Navigators were expected to attain a Morse proficiency of eight words per minute, and Oscar was grateful for his prescience in completing basic Morse training at the local Post Office, despite the fact that he had found it tedious at the time. Tuition was either six hours of lectures that lasted the entire day or three hours of flying with lectures filling the remaining hours. The total air time of the course varied between 60 and 80 hours, depending on the base and, inevitably, the weather. The trainees lived, studied and socialised together as one large group and Oscar was to quickly appreciate his three years as a boarder in college where he gained significant skills in assimilating within a large and diverse group.

For Oscar, Christmas 1942 represented a marked departure from the family affair that was Christmas 1941, which he had spent at home in Wentworth Falls. This time he would celebrate at the King Edward Hotel in Edmonton, Alberta, with two of his course mates, Walter Weekes, and Kenneth 'Snowy' Frost, from Oldham, England, who had enlisted in the RAAF. Oscar, Walter and Snowy enjoyed a long weekend at the King Edward, spending Christmas Day alternating between the hotel's coffee shop and the dining room.

The King Edward Hotel, Edmonton, Alberta, Canada (Peel Library, University of Alberta image).

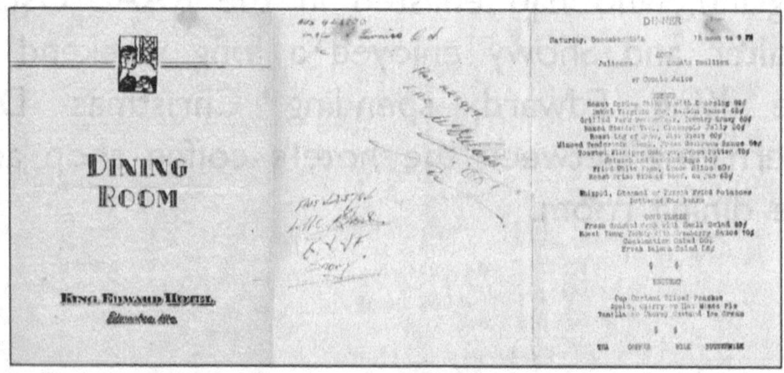


The King Edward Hotel dining room Christmas dinner menu. Dinner was served from 12.00 noon to 9.00 pm on Saturday 26 December (author image).

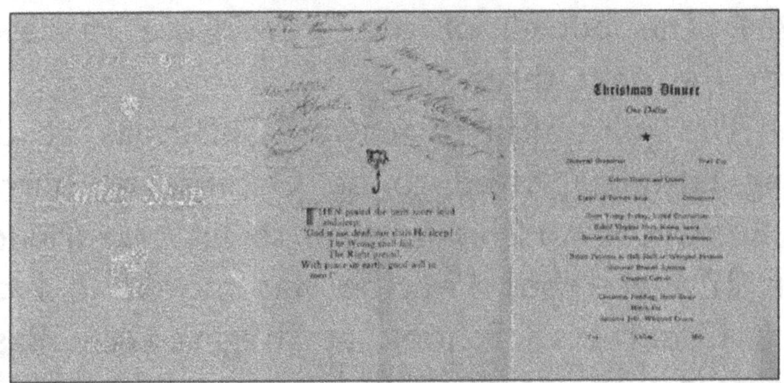
Christmas Dinner

The King Edward Hotel Christmas 1942 coffee shop menu. All this for the princely sum of $1.00 (author image).

Like Oscar, Walter Weekes trained as a navigator and was later posted to 460 Squadron. He would not survive the war, dying of injuries following an aircraft accident in which his Lancaster ME727 crashed just after take-off on a bombing mission on 9 April 1944, the day before Oscar was posted to 467 Squadron. Walter's father, a traveller for Wakefield Oil (Castrol), was notified of his son's death by telegram while he was travelling through Coonamble in New South Wales.

Snowy Frost was born in England, emigrated to Australia, enlisted in the RAAF and served in the RAF's 97 Squadron. Like Walter, he was not destined to survive, killed when the Lancaster bomber he was piloting crashed into the North Sea just off the coast of Norfolk during the flight home from a bombing mission on 24 September

1944. The bodies of the crew were retrieved over the next three days.

The jolly affair that was Christmas at the King Edward proved to be Oscar's last hurrah at Edmonton and his farewell to his two friends. On 27 December 1942 he was moved to No.3 Air Observers' School at Regina Air Base, Saskatchewan, some 800 kilometres south-east of Edmonton, and close to the beautiful, leafy city of Regina, with its broad boulevards and gracious buildings. His posting was to last four months and would see him complete his 20 weeks' training as a navigator. At Regina, Oscar was to complete more flying hours in an Avro Anson, a 'great uncle' to the Avro Lancaster he would later crew on operations over occupied Europe.

Twin-engine Avro Anson and its relatively simple controls, and a Taylor JT1 monoplane (author images).

In September 1942, No.3 Air Observers' School opened a detachment at Air Base Pearce in Alberta, the plan to eventually move all the air observers' courses the 600 kilometres from Regina to Pearce. However, the escalation of hostilities in the war in the Pacific saw a significant drop in the number of RAAF personal sent to Canada for training and the transfer was never completed, the decision eventually reversed. Nonetheless a number of courses were transferred to Pearce, notably those commencing on 12 December 1942 and 6 January 1943. Among the trainees to be transferred was Oscar Furniss, who left Regina with some regret to return to the broad, treeless countryside that surrounded Air Base Pearce. He was posted to No.66 Course at No.7 Service Flying Training School on 6 January 1943, and spent the next three months completing his final navigator courses.

The Canadian weather during the post-Christmas period in 1942-43 was among the bleakest on record. Given the enormous expanse that is the land mass of continental North America, the area hosts a variety of microclimates. Some indication of the weather Oscar would have endured during that bitterly cold winter is provided by a report describing conditions in Ontario, on the east coast, during that same period:

> Eastern Ontario's Freezing Rain Storm—December 28–30, 1942. Ice 'as thick as a person's wrist' covered telephone wires, trees and railway tracks. In Ottawa, 50,000 workers walked to work for five days. Because of the war there were fewer men available to clear the streets and repair lines.[10]

The aircrew curriculum devoted considerable time to the cross-training of crew members, part of the survival strategy to cope with an emergency during a mission. Many wireless operators were trained as air gunners, while the flight engineer was often informally trained by the pilot to fly the aircraft straight and level. For his part, the navigator taught the air gunner to calculate a simple course. Indeed, some navigators, including Oscar, were actually trained as reserve pilots, provided sufficient instruction to fly the bomber home should the pilot be wounded or killed. A number of navigators also completed extra training to gain experience before becoming operational.

On 15 April 1943, No.66 Course held a 'Wings Parade' at which the class of one Canadian and 25 RAAF trainees received their brevets (winged navigator insignia). Oscar would be just one of 699 RAAF personnel who graduated as navigators following training in Canada. In a move that brought them one step closer to their operational units in the UK, they were then posted to No.1 Y Depot at Halifax, on the beautiful island of Nova Scotia on the Atlantic coast, where they would wait for their transport to England.

Having graduated as a navigator, Oscar was promoted to temporary sergeant on 16 April 1943. Despite finally securing the precious navigator brevet Oscar, like many of his contemporaries, preferred to wear the observer brevet. The observer was multi-tasked and equipped with skills such as gunnery, and could perform the role of bomb aimer, wireless radio operator and also often had some flying experience. A navigator was simply trained to navigate.

Oscar's navigator brevet (author image).

The young airmen were to travel across the heart of Canada to Nova Scotia by train and were delighted to discover that, as a result of their recent promotion to sergeant, they were entitled to a Pullman carriage with its sleeping berth and porter. Oscar arrived in Halifax on 28 April 1943 after a 4700-kilometre train journey lasting four days.

No.1 Y Depot was an embarkation depot for sea transport to the UK, more a temporary address than a place of residence for the many thousands of RAAF personnel who passed through its doors. It was the centre of an operational transit point that served a number of eastern Canadian cities including Montreal and

Toronto. It was quite common for aircrew in transit to the UK to spend a month attached to the depot between their arrival on the east coast and embarkation on an escorted troopship, either from Halifax or New York.

'Old 'Y' Depot, Halifax' (R. Malcolm Warner, AWM ART24109).

On 2 May 1943 Oscar was transferred to his third air force, this time the RAF, prior to embarking for the UK. His embarkation date was set for 27 May 1943. He was granted three weeks' pre-embarkation leave from 3 May, the first three days of which, to his lasting regret, he spent in a Canadian air station hospital suffering from bronchitis. This was the first of several such hospitalisations, the remainder in

England, where he would be constantly plagued by bouts of bronchial and chest infections. His susceptibility to respiratory ailments was a matter of genetics—he had inherited it from the Furniss family.

However, possibly through a combination of meticulous medical treatment and sheer determination, Oscar recovered sufficiently to spend the remainder of his three-week leave period travelling and sightseeing. New York was one destination he was eager to visit and he sent his family a number of photographs taken in the biggest city he had ever seen. On 27 May 1943, his holiday over, Oscar rejoined his fellow graduates in Halifax for the train trip to New York, their embarkation point for the UK.

Bob Hunter was to arrive in New York a fortnight after Oscar sailed for Liverpool, and enjoyed almost three weeks of leave before embarking on the next fast ship sailing to the UK. Bob and Aub travelled widely around New York, also visiting several towns along the coast to Massachusetts. By the time Bob boarded the *Queen Elizabeth,* his bags were crammed with souvenirs, his pockets were empty and the Commanding Officer (CO) at Camp Myles Standish was pulling his hair out after 140 men disappeared—absent without leave—in one night. Unsurprisingly, all leave was subsequently cancelled. Bob's lasting impression of New York was the universal love of the local people for Australians and a cost of living that was three times that of Brisbane.

New York as Oscar saw it in May 1943 (Oscar Furniss image).

From New York, the young Australians joined a fast ship running the gauntlet of the U-boat 'wolf packs' in the dangerous voyage across the Atlantic to the UK. It was his second sea voyage and one that would take him even further from his family, his home, his native land and all he held dear. But, like the other young men who gathered in little knots on the decks and in the hallways, chatting and laughing, eventually lining the railings eager for their first glimpse of Britain, Oscar thought only of the life that awaited him and for which he had completed his first period of preparation. The next few months would truly test his mettle and reveal to his instructors, his superiors, and to Oscar himself whether he had the nerve to take the fight to the enemy in the skies over occupied Europe.

# CHAPTER 4

# ENGLAND WHILE THE SUN SHINES

Oscar's last sight of New York was sobering. Close to his embarkation point was the blackened hulk of the luxury French liner *Normandie,* lying on her side at Pier 88 after a devastating fire. The *Normandie* had been a magnificent vessel, fitted with Art Déco interiors and a vast dining room decorated with Lalique glass. Requisitioned by the US government to serve as a troopship, she caught fire during her conversion and was gutted by flames in a spectacular blaze initially denounced as the work of saboteurs. The *Normandie* lay on her side at her mooring for over a year as troopships filed past, a dire reminder to those who sailed towards the fields of battle of the flimsy nature of the craft that traversed the high seas.

Those memories would fade quickly as Oscar's ship ventured forth into the chilly waters of the Atlantic to complete a mercifully uneventful voyage before she docked at Liverpool on 4 June 1943. The young Australians disembarked, grateful to have arrived safely given the perils of crossing one of the most dangerous of the world's oceans at that time. They could not have known that, just three months earlier, the largest convoy battle of the war had been fought in the same stretch of the Atlantic they had just traversed. An Allied convoy of 110 ships, 13 escorts and several reinforcement vessels had been shadowed by a German wolf pack of 41 U-boats. As many as 38 U-boats had attacked the convoy, sinking 22 ships with the loss of 300 lives. A British Royal Navy report later admitted that 'The Germans never came so near to disrupting communications between the New World and the Old as in the first 20 days of March 1943.'[11] Such battles remained a closely guarded secret and the young trainee aircrew were perhaps fortunate that they were not privy to such secrets. It would have made for a nervous passage.

Stan Jolly made the same crossing a month later, describing his voyage after the war. Some weeks earlier Stan had seen the movie 'Action on the North Atlantic', starring Humphrey Bogart as the captain of a destroyer. His memory of the movie was that the ship seemed to spend more time under water than above. Stan woke after his first night at sea and was very pleased to find the ocean 'millpond smooth'. Compared to most troops on the ship, the Australians fared well, accommodated in a comfortable four-berth cabin with a freshwater shower. Like Oscar, Stan also sailed from New York to the UK, although his ship, the *Queen Elizabeth,* made the crossing in just six days, three days faster than any escorted convoy, the vessel's swifter crossing only possible because she had sailed unescorted, zigzagging across the North Atlantic. The risks of unescorted crossings were substantial, and they remained the province of the fast passenger liners that could outrun German torpedoes. The new 80,000-ton *Queen Elizabeth* and her sister ship, the *Queen Mary,* were two of just a handful of ships that were fast enough to cross unescorted. However, such crossings were certainly not for the faint-hearted.

Bob Hunter was on the next east-bound crossing of the *Queen Elizabeth* after Stan and was delighted to be farewelled by Red Cross ladies handing out donuts and lemon drinks on the wharf. He was also comfortably accommodated, albeit in a very cosy six-man cabin. With 18,000 troops on the ship, the galley was kept busy providing two hot meals a day to its large population of passengers. Bob's gratitude for his cabin was further increased when he noticed 25 Americans sleeping on a piece of deck space that measured around 10 feet square.

Having survived the most hazardous part of their journey, Oscar and his fellow aviators boarded a train at Liverpool Station, bound for No.11 Personnel Despatch and Receiving Centre in Brighton, where they had been instructed to report the following day, 5 June 1943. The Receiving Centre used both the Grand and Metropole hotels on the waterfront at Brighton as accommodation for incoming RAAF aircrew and these stately buildings must have presented an imposing sight with their grand façades. Indeed, two marble pillars in the reception area of the Grand Hotel still bear the initials, names and dates carved into them by transiting airmen during World War II.

Top: the Grand Hotel at Brighton during World War II (Grand Brighton Hotel image). Bottom: the Metropole Hotel (Hilton Brighton Metropole image).

Jack Colpus was accommodated in an older hotel known as the Bath Hotel:

> [W]e landed in Avonmouth near Bristol and went from there down to Brighton in the train ... Brighton is a seaside town, we were lucky we were billeted in an old hotel called the Bath Hotel. [W]hen I got my wings I also got a commission so I was a pilot officer and being an officer we got a bit of VIP treatment which was good. So we were billeted in this old Bath Hotel which was right on the sea front and ... It had ... a huge bath in the bedroom—it must

> have been about six foot long and huge taps in it. Turn the tap on and it ... would fill up the bath in no time so we enjoyed that. No showers of course and the meals were good. Everything was fine, it was good. The only thing that was a bit scary was German fighters used to come over and spray the town occasionally with bullets etc and they attacked one of the other hotels that was housing servicemen ... Yeah, they knew that we were there I'm sure. They picked out the hotels that had the servicemen in them. Their intelligence would be pretty good I should think.[12]

Oscar's destination was No.11 Personnel Despatch and Receiving Centre, an enormous transit point, a repository for aircrew until the RAF administration could process their postings to an advanced flying unit before they joined their operational units. Most proceeded to Bomber Command units, while others joined Fighter Command or Coastal Command. The administrative process could take several months to complete and many aircrew, itching to join their units, instead found themselves trapped in long periods of enforced idleness which could last up to three months. Mindful of this, the Receiving Centre pursued active programs designed to keep the waiting airmen occupied.

There was a daily routine of physical training and entertainment and the facilities of the beautiful coastal town of Brighton were available for the transiting aircrew, most on their first visit to England.

Brighton waterfront in 1941 was heavily defended against possible invasion. While the thought of staying in a luxury hotel on the beachfront might sound idyllic, the reality was somewhat different (image courtesy Metropole Hilton).

A number of men took the opportunity to visit relatives as, at that time, a large proportion of Australia's population still had strong family ties to the UK. Oscar embarked on a trip to the pretty little village of Riccall, in north Yorkshire, to visit the family's ancestral home.

There were also 'hospitality schemes' established by British societies aware of the large numbers of dominion servicemen who had travelled to the UK for wartime service. Conscious that many of these men had no family in Britain, such organisations as the Royal Empire Society recognised the need to assist these servicemen who were otherwise left to their own devices in a country with which they were largely unfamiliar. The Empire Societies' War Hospitality Committee was duly established under the auspices of the Royal Empire Society, and operated as an umbrella organisation for a large body of hospitality committees active both within the UK, including Scotland, Ireland and Wales, and as far afield as the East Indies, Africa and the West Indies. A Central Information Bureau offered servicemen a canteen and recreation facilities, introductions to clubs, advice on lodging and dining, and sightseeing tours. These were open to both men and women of all ranks. A helpful pamphlet listed the locations of leave centres scattered throughout the UK, describing the facilities available and any charges that applied. A map was included to assist the serviceman in locating the centre.

Oscar's ancestral home at Riccall in Yorkshire (author image).

One popular service involved the provision of a family home environment to visit during periods of leave. The Dominion Officers' and Students' Hospitality Scheme, established by Lady Frances Ryder and Miss Macdonald, put commissioned officers in touch with families who would host them during their leave periods. Many of these families had their own young men serving close to the front and were delighted to look after dominion officers who were so far from home.

Despite the kindness of the British people, life at the Receiving Centre could be monotonous and frustrating for young men desperate to see some action after months of training.

Complicating the posting cycle was the fact that, in early 1942, the RAF had decided to dispense with the second pilot on heavy bombers due to the increasing shortage of pilots in Bomber Command units. Even given these continuing shortages, by late 1943 pilots could wait at Brighton for up to four months before being posted to an advanced flying unit. Colin Dickson, later to command Oscar's Lancaster aircrew, would sit around the Receiving Centre for two months while Bomber Command units pleaded for more pilots. For those who dreamt of flying a Spitfire there was even less prospect of a call-up as single-engine pilots were in far less demand at this stage of the war. Indeed, at that time, Fighter Command had 945 more pilots than aircraft.

Colin Dickson's decision to join the RAAF was a natural extension of his service in the militia. When Colin enlisted in January 1939 the constitutional restriction that prevented the militia serving overseas was not an issue as war was still eight months away. Once war broke out, Colin had the option of transferring to the AIF, which was not encouraged by a military keen to prevent the movement of large numbers of men from the militia, or joining the RAAF. Colin was a qualified electrician and demonstrated a natural affinity for all things mechanical. His skills would see him become a pilot of exceptional ability.

Having finally been processed by the RAF administrative behemoth, those men who, like Oscar, were destined for Bomber Command, were sent to pre-squadron training at advanced flying units. There, navigators in particular began to learn that there was an enormous difference between plotting courses in the broad expanse of Canadian prairie that surrounded Air Base Pearce and the far more varied topography of Britain with its rugged, mountainous spine, its lush, rolling hills and patchwork farmland, and its urban and semi-urban cityscapes.

Jack Colpus was grateful for the time spent acclimatising to the English countryside. While he had trained in Western Australia rather than Canada, the contrast with the English countryside was similarly stark:

> [I had] to familiarise myself with the English countryside because the English countryside is altogether different from Australia. There's no huge paddocks—there were all these tiny little fields as they called them, surrounded by hedges and they're all different colours from brown to green and yellow if they've got the rape growing and a real picture actually. Like a ... bedspread, a patchwork bedspread. Really altogether

> different from Australia and the roads, the towns, everything's so close together compared to Australia ... [In] Cunderdin town you've got railway lines zigzagging all over the place and tiny rivers so you had to virtually learn to map read again so one of the things that we did was map reading and generally getting to acclimatise ourselves with the situation of the different temperatures and ... the fact that the stars in the northern hemisphere are different to the southern hemisphere.[13]

Australian airman Les Jubbs also wrote of the initial shock of flying over topography that was vastly different to anything he had previously experienced:

> In Brighton, daily postings to RAF stations would be announced ... One of the first postings was often to an Elementary Flying Training School to once again fly Tiger Moths. Immediate response was disappointment but being brought up to the reality of flying from an airfield close to London where, once you took off and viewed the countryside with its enormous range of topical details was mind boggling. The wide expanse of Australian landscape was in marked contrast to what was now beheld. Multi railway tracks running in all

> directions, multitude of roads, towns, villages and fields of green were before them in a confusing abundance.
>
> Map reading was paramount if a pilot wasn't to become easily lost [and] ... to become very familiar with the immediate area around the [Elementary Flying Training School]. Venturing away was for another day and that was usually on short excursions to nearby villages or towns. This in reality was a great introduction to what flying in the British Isles could be really like especially in these hugely built up areas near London.[14]

The weather was another factor altogether. Those like Oscar who had trained in Canada had become used to a climate which was characterised by extremes largely predicted by the seasons. The damp British climate, particularly close to the English Channel, often saw the countryside mired in mist, rain and low clouds, making flying either hazardous in the extreme or nigh on impossible. Pilots were rapidly forced to learn to land an aircraft on instruments in the thick, soupy fog that Britons know so well.

Oscar remained in Brighton, cooling his heels at the Receiving Centre and anxious to resume his journey to Bomber Command. He enjoyed several days' leave in late June, the English countryside at its best under the warmth of the summer sun, the trees clad in bright green summer foliage, encouraging outdoor excursions such as boating or picnicking. Returning to the Receiving Centre to resume the interminable waiting must have been difficult and engendered feelings of frustration, disillusionment and perhaps even depression. Les Jubbs noted that the waiting aircrew were also taunted by glimpses of aircraft setting off on missions in the skies above:

> ...every day they could witness very large flights of USA Flying Fortresses departing for Europe at great heights but only evidenced by the long vapour trails showing their presence. Hours later many of these aircraft would come staggering back across the coast at low altitude where silent engines were plainly evident indicating badly damaged aircraft.
>
> Some reality of the war in the air was there for RAAF aircrews to come to grips with, but no such evidence was to be seen regarding the RAF armadas that set forth on night bombing missions. Enormous losses were suffered every night on these missions yet details were not available to the public. Any reports, either by radio, newspapers, or cinema newsreels were greatly censored and only positives promulgated.

> This was the environment that these young men found themselves in and a certain amount of concern crept into their minds as to what purpose they had come 12,000 miles. Some would find themselves in operational squadrons acting in an air traffic control capacity, but often in a minor role. This situation often drifted on for many months so some would seek out how best they could be better employed while others happened to be in the right place at the right time to hear about other capacities they could volunteer such as glider pilots or flight engineer.[15]

However the young Australians had no choice but to simply endure the wait, seeking whatever diversions they could to pass the time. The RAF appeared conscious of the fact that there were numbers of young dominion aircrew idling at Brighton and occasionally resorted to unusual schemes to alleviate the boredom. Les Jubbs described an extraordinary training course that was offered to the dominion aircrew waiting with him in Brighton:

> There was a stirring of malcontent among these young eager pilots, which was temporarily stifled when many were sent on a Commando Course to Whitely Bay. There it was mentioned that there was

every possibility they would be sent to far away Burma and this training was essential for survival in that tropical environment. [There were no trees at Whitely Bay].[16]

Oscar himself appears to have been sent on one of these more unusual training exercises from 2 to 14 July 1943 when he was posted to the 34th Tank Brigade. He must have greeted news of his movement to a tank brigade with some astonishment given the extraordinary disconnect between tanks and aircraft. The 34th Tank Brigade was raised in July 1941 and spent the next three years training in southern England before deploying to France as part of the Normandy bridgehead following the D Day landings on 6 June 1944. While it is difficult to understand why aircrew would have been posted to an armoured unit, the 34th certainly conducted battle courses that could have provided valuable training for aircrew. The airmen had received little or no basic infantry training and their time at the armoured brigade could have seen them hone their weapons skills and complete training in concealment and evasion. Airmen shot down over France were often picked up by the French resistance and moved between a series of safe houses before they could be safely returned to England. At the very least, they needed to know how to defend themselves and avoid capture by the Germans. Should it prove difficult for the local resistance cell to arrange a safe passage home, the airman might find himself fighting as a member of the Maquis, armed guerrilla fighters who waged a hit-and-run campaign against the Germans from bases hidden in the forests.

Another explanation for Oscar's posting to the 34th Tank Brigade could have been disarmingly simple. The RAF could have viewed this as a means to provide variety for the aircrew, to fill directing staff vacancies for 34th Brigade exercises and to free up accommodation in Brighton for incoming aircrew. Whatever the reason, the posting period certainly provided some variation in activity and exposed aircrew such as Oscar to the work of the other arms and services.

On 2 August 1943, after almost two months of enforced idleness in Brighton, Oscar finally received news of his posting to an advanced flying unit. He was officially posted to No.9 Observers Advanced Flying Unit at Llandwrog in north Wales, where he would complete a four-week course. Here Oscar would meet Stan Jolly, who was to become his aircrew bomb aimer.

Llandwrog sits on the north-western coast of Wales, some eight kilometres south of the major Welsh town of Caernarfon and is a tiny, compact village of stone cottages and a public house. Its name, Llandwrog, means 'Church of Saint Twrog', and refers to the village's magnificent medieval stone church with its elegant spire. RAF Base Llandwrog sits just behind the beach, another four kilometres beyond the village. The beach is on Caernarfon Bay, which is part of the Irish Sea and has a major impact on the local climate. Good weather in this area usually lasts around three to four weeks at the beginning of summer, from June through July. In 1943, according to Stan Jolly, summer lingered into late July and the aircrew enjoyed cricket games in the warm weather, the equipment and whites supplied by the RAF.[17] The base also lay in the shadow of Mt Snowden, the highest point in the British Isles south of Hadrian's Wall. At 1085 metres, it is dwarfed by many of the mountains in Europe, but was sufficiently lofty to pose a threat to aircraft flown by trainee crews.

During its period of operations, RAF Llandwrog was the busiest airfield in Wales. It was home to an air gunnery school, a navigation training school, an air wireless operator school and a bomb aimer school, all of which used Avro Anson aircraft. Oscar was attached to the navigation school during his time in Llandwrog and would acquire around 30 hours of air time in navigation exercises over both land and water.

Llandwrog airfield, viewed from the west and looking north-east, is surrounded by water on three sides, including the tempestuous Irish Sea (bottom edge of the photo). The triangular layout of the runway provided more flight direction options during inclement weather. Despite this, conditions for pilots attempting to take off and land were challenging, particularly in the lightweight Avro Anson (Heritage Studio 81 image).

A core role of the advanced flying units was to train navigators and radio operators to work as a team. The wireless operator would obtain navigation information in Morse Code from beacons and relay this to the navigator. The navigator would then confirm their position by reckoning, either by plot or calculation. A secondary role was to provide the many aircrew who had trained overseas in such locations as sunny Australia or Canada with their vast expanses of territory, experience in British flying conditions. These conditions featured climatic characteristics such as fog and rain, and wartime hazards such as barrage balloons, blackouts and crowded skies. The aircrew also had to become accustomed to long winter nights and long summer days. England operated on two hours of daylight saving in summertime when darkness did not fall until after 10.00 pm.

Oscar was also exposed to a number of specific aircraft manoeuvres during his training at the advanced flying unit, including the defensive movement known as the 'corkscrew'. This manoeuvre saw the aircraft spiral down for perhaps 1000 feet, turn and climb again to regain height, repeating the sequence as necessary. Its purpose was to shake off a pursuing German *Luftwaffe* fighter. The corkscrew was just one of many manoeuvres the aircrew learned during training that had the potential to save their lives on operations. Oscar was to revisit this exhilarating manoeuvre in March 1944 at RAF Winthorpe when Colin Dickson would fling the more obsolete Stirling bomber into a corkscrew manoeuvre on several terrifying occasions during training at No.1661 Heavy Conversion Unit.

Stan Jolly had been training as an observer in Australia and North America, but had recently remustered. While waiting in Brighton in July he had been advised that Bomber Command had a surplus of navigators but a shortage of bomb aimers. Stan remustered to bomb aimer and was posted to RAF Penrhos in northern Wales on 27 July. After a fortnight Stan's group moved to join Oscar and his fellow airmen at Llandwrog, as there were no night flying facilities at RAF Penrhos.

On 31 August 1943 Oscar and Stan were both transferred from RAF Llandwrog to No.27 Operational Training Unit at RAF Lichfield, 32 kilometres north of Birmingham in the Midlands. Here they were to complete a conversion course from pre-war training aircraft such as the Avro Anson to the modern, heavy Wellington bombers. The Operational Training Unit was also the place where the disparate collection of individuals would be welded into tightly knit teams as the future crews of heavy bombers.

Remaining buildings at RAF Lichfield include two hangers behind a flood levee (top) and the operations building (author images).

The guardhouse at the front entrance to RAF Lichfield has been preserved and appears much as it did in Oscar's time.

Lichfield also has a brick wall that was used for zeroing the machine-guns on the Wellington bombers and which still bears a faint rondel high up on its face. Soft-nosed bullets were used to avoid destroying the wall (author images).

The day that set the path for Oscar's future was 2 September 1943. Once all the trainee aircrew were settled in their barracks, they assembled in the base hall and the pilots were asked to select their crew. It was not unlike selecting a team for a football or cricket match, albeit with far more serious implications. A pilot's first priority was to choose the best navigator available as he was the key to finding both the target and, importantly, the way home.

The man who would pilot Oscar Furniss' aircraft was 422038 Flight Sergeant Colin Dickson, an electrician from Kempsey in New South Wales. Dickson immediately chose Oscar as his navigator, a measure of Oscar's impressive performance on the course. Dickson then chose Bob Hunter as his wireless operator and Stan Jolly as his gunner/bomb aimer. Next he chose 424403 Flight Sergeant Hilton Forden, a clerk from Newcastle, New South Wales, as his rear gunner. These men comprised the core crew of five; Colin Dickson would later select the extra crew he needed, choosing men with the skills required for the type of aircraft they would fly. Ultimately the crew would serve on Lancaster bombers and, once that decision was made, Colin chose a flight engineer and mid-upper gunner, both members of the RAF Volunteer Reserve.

Colin Dickson was the only crew member with previous military experience, having served in the militia as a member of the 13th Infantry Battalion between January 1939 and April 1942. The oldest of the all-Australian crew was 22, the youngest, just 19. At 160 centimetres, Stan Jolly was the shortest crew member. It would be almost two weeks before they would take off on their first flight together as a crew.

Bomber Command squadrons flew a number of different aircraft. Oscar's crew would train initially on the Vickers Wellington, a twin-engine heavy bomber with a crew of six, recently increased from five in an attempt to improve bombing accuracy.

The new crew in London, December 1943. Standing (left to right): Bob Hunter, Colin Dickson, Hilton Forden. Squatting (left to right): Stan Jolly, Oscar Furniss (Jolly family image).

The Vickers Wellington Bomber without its fabric skin, photographed at Brooklands where it was constructed. The geodesic/triangular construction of its fuselage made it extremely strong, able to withstand an enormous amount of structural damage and still fly home. This particular bomber was recovered from Loch Ness.

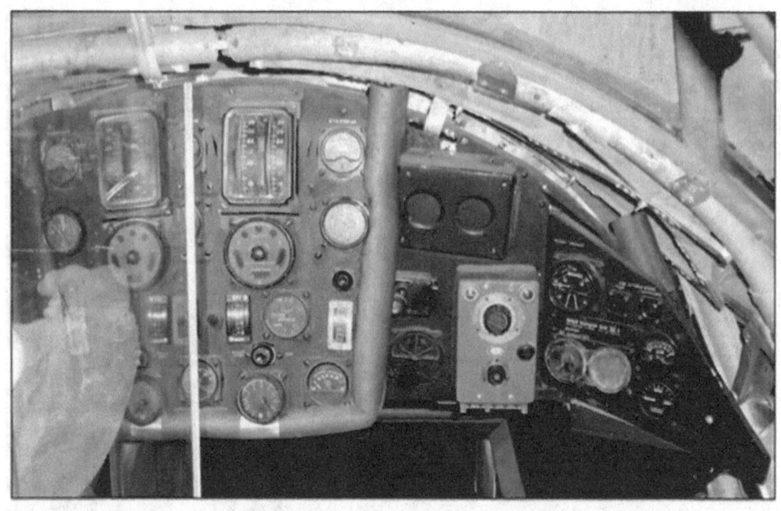

The instrument panel of the Wellington was far more complex than that of the Avro Anson, although much less complicated than that of the Lancaster (author images).

Following a two-week period of classroom instruction, the crew spent the next seven weeks flying, honing their skills, familiarising themselves with the aircraft and moulding themselves into a well-drilled team. They were granted access to top secret information and warned so sternly about the penalties for its disclosure, accidental or otherwise that, as Bob Hunter wrote later, they were not prepared to record it in written form. They were also given extra tuition in the skills of evasion should they be shot down over occupied territory. Testing these skills took the form of a practical exercise that saw them dropped 25 kilometres from Lichfield with 6d (five cents) in their pockets. They were told to make their own way back to the base using their wits and whatever resources came to hand.

On Monday 20 September, the crew had its first training flight in a Wellington. They performed routine manoeuvres known as 'circuits and bumps', designed to provide pilot Colin Dickson his first experience at the controls of the heavy bomber. From then on, they took the aircraft up daily on routine circuits, averaging two to three hours' flying time.

Flying at Lichfield was not without its dangers, particularly from the winged inhabitants of nearby Coventry Canal. On one memorable day, a flock of birds flew into a Wellington as it was taking off. One of the propellers was shattered and the young pilot managed a half-circuit of the aerodrome before crash-landing in a far corner. Fortuitously, all the crew escaped unscathed.

On 1 October 1943 the crew members set off on their first cross-country night flight. Predictably, they lost their way, although in Oscar's defence, there was heavy cloud cover, rated as 10/10 by the crew. If nothing else, this experience demonstrated the importance of visual landmark recognition. However, during this early training period, the crew partnership that mattered most was between pilot and navigator, while the crewman under closest scrutiny was usually the radio operator. His skills at using Morse Code, his ability to use a variety of radios, his understanding of the signals he received from the various transmitters and the clarity of his broadcasts were all subject to almost forensic examination.

One of the quirks of the Wellington was that the front gunner/bomb aimer was shut into his turret by another crew member, usually the navigator. Stan Jolly hated this arrangement, aware that his life was in Oscar's hands, and hoping fervently that, if the aircraft was hit, Oscar would survive long enough to free him from the front turret. The door of the turret had to be closed to minimise the draught blowing through the aircraft from the gun apertures in the front turret. The Lancasters had a door behind the radio operator for the same purpose. Arthur 'Bomber' Harris also clearly disliked this arrangement and it became another of the changes he introduced soon after his appointment as Commander-in Chief of Bomber Command in February 1942.

Apart from the nerve-racking prospect of being locked in the bomb aimer's compartment, Stan enjoyed Lichfield. A secondary role for the bomb aimer in the Wellington was as a 'spare' pilot, taking over the controls to allow the other crew members time to prepare to bale out. This required Stan to spend around an hour a day in a Link Trainer, an aircraft simulator, and perhaps to imagine that his earlier ambition to train as a pilot had been realised after all. Stan also enjoyed time on the range at Lichfield and his gunnery performance was rated as above average. This compensated for his below average rating on the one bomb he dropped at Llandwrog, which Stan argued unsuccessfully had a faulty tail.

By October 1943 Oscar's health had begun to break down and the serious chest infection that had seen him hospitalised in Canada now returned with a vengeance. On 3 October, at the end of the day's flight, Oscar stumbled across to the station sick quarters at RAF Lichfield, suffering a persistent, hacking cough and wracked by fever. He was immediately admitted to hospital for three days' bed rest, the crew's cross-country flights cancelled for the period of his absence.

While Oscar was clearly susceptible to bronchitis, smoking was also a major factor. Like many of his peers, Oscar was a heavy smoker. Among his personal effects later returned to his family were four cigarette cases and three pipes. This was a common trait among men of that era and, while occasionally they were advised to stop smoking given the recurrence of chest infections, few did.

However, Oscar was young and determined and desperate to return to flying, and he recovered quickly. On 16 October 1943 he was promoted to temporary flight sergeant and added a crown to his sergeant's chevrons. This promotion must have been doubly welcome as it formally recognised his qualification as an operational navigator. A day later, his luck ran out, his bronchitis caught up with him again and he was readmitted to hospital. The English weather clearly did not agree with him and he was to fight a constant battle to ward off chest infections. This time he was in hospital for nine days and the crew simply had to continue flight training without him. He returned to training on 27 October ready to resume the almost daily routine of circuits flying the Wellington.

Flight training could be hazardous for the young trainee crews and Lichfield was by no means exempt from tragic accidents. On Saturday 6 November, a calm, clear night, four aircraft were lost in separate incidents. One of the 24 men killed shared Oscar's accommodation hut, his death plunging the men into a period of gloom and despondency. They were to realise quickly that the loss of fellow crewmen was simply an occupational hazard and one they had to learn to endure, mustering all their resilience to continue their training without the luxury of time to grieve.

Four nights later Oscar and his crew were involved in an exercise of a different kind. The operation involved a flight over the Irish Sea with a live 500lb bomb and four dummy bombs. The exercise was designed to familiarise the crew with the carriage of bombs and allow them to adjust to the additional weight of the aircraft. They manoeuvred with the bombs for the duration of the exercise and were then to bring them home intact rather than drop them. The operation proceeded to plan until they began their final landing run, only to find that the undercarriage had not locked and they were in danger of losing the 500lb bomb as they landed, with catastrophic consequences for them and the base. They were forced to abort the landing and divert to Church Broughton where they landed at 'crash stations', amid 'bags of panic' as Bob Hunter wrote later.[18]

On 17 November Oscar was promoted to substantive flight sergeant, just as his time at Lichfield was drawing to a close. One of the last exercises the crew completed before they left Lichfield involved their first 'semi-operational trip'. On the night of 25 November they flew across the English Channel to a point opposite the north-west coast of France, studying the coastline from the air and entering the airspace over occupied territory for the first time. It was a happily uneventful trip, all the men aware that this would by no means be typical of future trips over occupied France.

During their time at Lichfield the crew of five had accumulated over 48 hours of daylight flying and a further 38 hours of night-flying experience. It would be another six weeks before they flew again. In the meantime, the men were treated to 16 days of well-deserved leave.

The crew members decided to take their leave together and set off on 30 November to explore London, staying at the Victoria League Club off Edgware Road. After months of intense training, the men were ready to relax. Queenslander Stan Jolly wrote in his diary:

> Saw snow falling, toured the Houses of Parliament and the House of Commons. Then Westminster Abbey and the Boomerang Club, which operated out of Australia House for Aussie service personnel, Noel Coward's play 'Blythe Spirit' in the evening.[19]

The Boomerang Club was a social meeting place for Australian service personnel in London, operated from the basement of Australia House in The Strand. There Australian servicemen and women could dine, read somewhat out-of-date

Australian newspapers and arrange sightseeing around London.

The young airmen were also exposed to the true impact of the blitz, experiencing several air raids by the *Luftwaffe* and, like many Londoners, seeking refuge in an underground tube station among commuters and others caught out by the raids. The calmness of these people during air raids was a revelation to the Australians. For many Londoners, this was simply part of their lives and large numbers slept on the underground railway platforms each night for safety. The ability of the British to continue with their daily routine amid the destruction and frequent loss of life that were common features of the blitz was inspirational, the aircrew noting that even the daily changing of the guard at Buckingham Palace continued throughout the blitz. Like the Londoners themselves, the Australians took the wartime dangers in their stride, dancing, partying, dining out and gradually learning to relax again after the intensity of their training. Conscious that they would be posted to an operational squadron in the near future, they were determined to enjoy themselves as much as possible in the cosmopolitan vastness and colourful excitement of London.

On 15 December 1943 the crew returned from leave to be greeted by the news that they had been posted to Headquarters 51 Base at RAF Swinderby. RAF Swinderby sits close to the village of Swinderby and some 13 kilometres north-east of Newark-on-Trent, Nottinghamshire, alongside the road to Lincoln in Lincolnshire. A number of RAF substations were attached to RAF Swinderby, including RAF Scampton. The area is close to the east coast, with just the narrow waters of the English Channel separating it from German-occupied France.

The crew reported to RAF Swinderby just as the bitter English winter was setting in. The freezing cold chilled them to the bone and they were astonished at the sight of overhead wires thick with ice. The station itself was a temporary establishment and the Australian crewmen regarded it as rather underwhelming.

Two hangars are all that now remain of RAF Swinderby (author image).

Having arrived at Swinderby, the young Australians were immediately informed that they were to be attached to RAF Scampton from 20 December and were granted another 14 days' leave over the Christmas period. At that time RAF Scampton was in the process of a major upgrade, its grass runways re-laid with concrete to a thickness of 800 millimetres in the middle sections in preparation for training with heavy bombers. The additional leave presented something of a conundrum for some of the crew who were now fast running out of money, having not budgeted for another two weeks in London.

However there was no denying the allure of Christmas Eve in the English capital, particularly as the Australian High Commission had organised Christmas dinner and a concert at the Boomerang Club. In a seasonal tradition, the young airmen were served dinner by high-ranking officers and other dignitaries, including the Australian High Commissioner, former Prime Minister Stanley Bruce.

Christmas 1943 at the Boomerang Club. The Christmas Eve party was broadcast to Australia by the BBC Overseas Service program 'Radio Newsreel' on Christmas morning. Eight hundred members of the Australian forces attended the event and ate their way through 22 turkeys, 11 hams and a similarly large number of plum puddings (AWM SUK13318).

On 29 December 1943 the crew finally paraded at RAF Scampton where the men would remain for a month. RAF Scampton is located some 10 kilometres north of Lincoln and was previously home to 617 Squadron, the 'Dambusters' squadron. Scampton was a substantial base, consisting of four large hangars with permanent brick buildings and a number of aerodrome facilities constructed behind the hangars, the site occupying a considerable area. It boasted a sizeable collection of buildings for messing and quarters and well-appointed and comfortable accommodation for officers and airmen.

While life at RAF Scampton was far more comfortable than at Lichfield, the men discovered that they would not fly for the duration of their posting. Instead they would attend lectures for a period of four weeks, spending their entire time in the classroom. In between lectures they were left to their own devices, although the RAF provided a number of avenues for them to break the boredom and endless inactivity. Oscar and his crew played hockey, their sticks, pads and uniforms supplied by the RAF. As always, however, they were at the mercy of the weather, with one game abandoned after fog rolled in, completely obscuring the goal posts from view. There were also opportunities to study by correspondence and Stan Jolly took an accountancy course to fill the time and boost his qualifications for his post-war career.

Their proximity to the city of Lincoln was also an advantage and many of the airmen spent their free time exploring this historic city with its magnificent castle and medieval cathedral. Some of the other aircrew rented lodgings in the city so that they could escape the base during non-operational periods. On some RAF bases, the wives of aircrew lived close by, which was not always an advantage as Frederick Rosier, CO 229 Squadron, RAF, wrote later:

> When I went to Northolt I found that the wives of some of the chaps were living in the vicinity. It wasn't long before I stopped chaps living out and I said it would be far better if their wives moved away. It was affecting morale in that these wives would count the number of aeroplanes leaving and the number of aeroplanes coming back. And they were on the telephone to find out whether Willie was all right. It was far better when we were all living together in the mess and developing a first-class squadron spirit.[20]

Renting lodgings in the city was certainly not an option for Oscar and his crew who were now running seriously short of cash. They spent an uncharacteristically quiet New Year in camp, pooling their resources and opting for a home-made 'banquet' of sorts.

Lincoln Cathedral dominates the English east coast landscape. It was left undamaged by the *Luftwaffe* during the war for the simple reason that German pilots, like those of the RAF, used it as a navigation aid. For RAF bomber crews returning after a 10-hour raid into Germany, the spires of Lincoln Cathedral, either piercing the clouds or glistening in the sunlight, signalled their safe return.

Lincoln Cathedral, a welcoming sight for airmen returning from Germany (image courtesy of Don Hiller).

On 2 February 1944 the crew bade farewell to Scampton and moved to RAF Winthorpe where they were posted to No.52 Base Aircrew School, 1661 Heavy Conversion Unit. The task of the heavy conversion unit was to convert crews from the twin-engine Wellingtons to the four-engine Stirling or Lancaster bombers. At the time the base was equipped with a number of the somewhat obsolete Stirling bombers. Crews received flying training and ground training on alternate days, the entire course lasting six weeks.

RAF Winthorpe sits on the edge of the village of Newark-on-Trent, Nottinghamshire. During World War II there were over 80 operational airfields in this area and the conglomeration of airfields made the role of the navigator both complicated and crucial. It was no longer a matter of using visual reckoning to find three runways in a triangular layout as most airfields used a similar runway layout. It was not uncommon for aircraft to land at the wrong base. Navigators quickly realised that learning to recognise the local forests from the air would pay handsome dividends; while the triangular three-runway airfields that dotted the countryside all looked similar, the forests were unique in shape and size.

In one nerve-racking incident on 19 November 1943, a pilot from 467 Squadron was attempting to land a Lancaster bomber at RAF Waddington while talking to the RAF Cranwell tower. RAF Waddington was in a state of panic because its controllers could see a bomber trying to land but could not communicate with the pilot who was on the wrong radio frequency. This was 467 Squadron's first operational day from Waddington and marked an inauspicious start.

One of the idiosyncrasies of Winthorpe was a small hillock which sat just off line, at the end of one runway. While pilots were warned to watch for this mound, a number came to grief, catching the top of the mound either while struggling to lift off the ground or attempting a difficult landing.

Winthorpe was also often required to supply emergency crewmen to the surrounding squadrons at short notice. Some of those who were nearing the completion of their training were selected and occasionally these men never returned to finish their course.

Mid-air incidents were not uncommon. In one particularly nasty accident a Lancaster flew into the tow rope between another bomber and its glider. The Lancaster was 'cut in half' and all the crew were lost. Of the 125,000 men who served in Bomber Command during the war, 55,000 were to lose their lives. Some 7000 of these would die in training accidents.

Newark Air Museum memorial to aircrew killed during training at 1661 Heavy Conversion Unit at RAF Winthorpe (author image).

Plaque, Airmen's Chapel, Lincoln Cathedral (author image).

At RAF Winthorpe Colin Dickson submitted his application for commissioning to pilot officer. Commissioning was offered to those trainee pilots who finished in the top three of their course, suggesting that Colin was clearly a talented pilot. At the same time, the Australians met the two men who would complete the crew of seven for a heavy bomber. Philip ('Taffy') Weaver, a 33-year-old clerk from Llansamlet, South Wales, was the flight engineer, while Horace ('Jack') Skellorn, from Manchester, would be the mid-upper gunner, sitting exposed in a Perspex bubble that crouched limpet-like on the upper skin of the fuselage.

As British citizens, both these young men had a National Service obligation to fulfil. For Philip 'Taffy' Weaver, joining the RAF as a flight engineer was a natural extension of his work as a control room operator for the local gas authority. Taffy was fascinated by mechanics and constantly drew detailed diagrams of the machines with which he worked to increase his understanding of their function and the intricacy of their component parts. Jack Skellorn's enlistment in the RAF was prompted by his childhood idolisation of his uncle, who was a RAF air gunner. The first time the 16-year-old Jack saw his uncle's air gunner brevet, he decided that he would follow his uncle into the RAF should he be called up. Jack's greatest concern was that the war would be over before he was old enough to serve. For the rest of his life, Jack's uncle would hold himself responsible for his nephew's enlistment in the RAF and his subsequent death.

Engineer Taffy Weaver was a late starter, his time in an aircraft commencing on 30 January 1944 at 1661 Heavy Conversion Unit. Taffy's earlier training had consisted entirely of ground-based lectures and work with engines in stationary installations. His first flight with Oscar and his crew was on 8 March. Jack Skellorn had been at Lichfield at the same time as Oscar and his comrades and probably socialised with the Australian crew. Colin Dickson's was the fifth crew with whom Jack had flown in his first fortnight at 1661 Heavy Conversion Unit.

P. Weaver (F. Eng)

R. J. Hunter W/Op AG

Oscar S. Furniss (Nav.)

H Skellorn (MUAG)

C. Dickson (Pilot)

H H Forden (RG)

S D Jolly B.A.

The crew, now at its full complement of seven, stand under their obsolete Stirling bomber at RAF Winthorpe in March 1944. Left to right: Stan Jolly, Hilton Forden, Colin Dickson, Horace 'Jack' Skellorn, Oscar Furniss, Bob Hunter, Phil 'Taffy' Weaver. The reverse of this photo is signed by all seven airmen (Skellorn photo).

Over the next two weeks the crew flew in a mixture of combinations, with pilot Colin Dickson flying as second pilot or in command and the crew itself variously under supervision as the men honed their drills and familiarised themselves with their new crew members. Once the crew's final composition was confirmed, the men were granted a 48-hour leave pass. This was followed by a day at RAF Cranwell for 'dingy training'. This training comprised a practice rescue after ditching into water (in their case the English Channel), and was completed in the base's heated swimming pool. The drill emulated landing in water wearing a parachute and then climbing into a rescue dingy after releasing the parachute harness but while still wearing a full flying suit, now filled with water. For some airmen, the dingy training in the heated pool represented their first swim since leaving home. By this time, the ground had been covered in snow for six weeks.

The crew's greatest complaint about Winthorpe concerned heating: there was just one pot belly stove to heat their hut and their clothes were never completely dry. This may have been one of the factors in Oscar's recurring respiratory complaints. Crews arriving at a station always raced to secure the beds closest to the heater. One of the regular activities at Winthorpe that was not listed in the flying manual was shovelling snow, a constant and tedious chore in the depths of winter. But the snow was far less dangerous than the fog which could completely obscure the runway and provide high drama for aircrew returning from an exercise

It would be almost two weeks before the crew members completed their first flight in a Stirling, a bomber that many considered too outdated for operational flying. The men spent days completing circuits and landings, cross-country flying and dummy bombing runs, mixing this training with practising the 'corkscrew' manoeuvre designed to deny an enemy fighter a clear and stable target. The manoeuvre relied on fine judgement, commencing at the moment the fighter was assessed as ready to launch its attack. At this point, the pilot would fling the bomber into a series of violent changes in direction and altitude to dodge the incoming attack and in the hope of throwing the fighter off target so successfully that an attack would be abandoned. In total the crew completed over 24 hours of daytime flying and some 17 hours of night flying.

On 19 March 1944 the crew was transferred to No.5 Lancaster Finishing School at RAF Syerston in Nottinghamshire for a two-week conversion course from Stirling to Lancaster bombers. They greeted their departure from the outdated Stirlings with more than a little relief. RAF Syerston sits 12 kilometres south-west of Newark, and was home to the two Polish bomber squadrons during the war. The aircrew quarters were now located in a proper barracks block with central heating and a drying room. The crew members were delighted with their change of situation and enjoyed their brief time at Syerston.

Stan Jolly in the snow at RAF Winthorpe. The mass of a snowed-in wooden hut is just visible above the snowline in the background. Snow was a novel experience for Queenslanders Stan Jolly and Bob Hunter (Jolly family image).

RAF Syerston control tower (Milborne One image).

The crew was now training to fly the ultimate World War II heavy bomber, the four-engine Avro Lancaster. By this time Oscar had amassed over two years of flying training in Australia, Canada, Wales and England. His training had encompassed far more than simple navigation, also including meteorology, anti-gas warfare, bombing theory, hygiene and sanitation, the principles of flight, signals, law, discipline, administration, and training in armaments from machine-guns and ammunition to the various types of bombs.

As a navigator, Oscar would also be trained in the use of the new navigation systems introduced during the war. These included the

Gee system, developed by the RAF, which worked on measuring the time delay between two radio signals to determine the location of the aircraft. The system was accurate to within a few hundred metres and had a range exceeding 550 kilometres. Another new system was the H2S, nicknamed 'STINK'. This system was also developed by the RAF and comprised an aircraft-mounted, ground-reading radar. It used elementary electronic target identification to assist navigation and bombing, thus extending the accuracy of target location well beyond the range of the Gee system. The third system in which Oscar would certainly have been trained was known as 'Oboe'. Also developed in wartime, Oboe projected a beam, slightly more than 30 metres wide, along which the aircraft flew. It was limited to use by one aircraft at a time and was eventually replaced by the Gee system. German radar could detect this beam and named it according to the mark it left on radar screens—'boomerang'.

Following their first one-hour familiarisation, most of the crew's flights at Syerston were less than two hours in duration and, again, consisted primarily of circuits and landings, with the occasional cross-country flight. During their time at Syerston they accumulated over eight hours of daylight and more than seven hours of night flying. On one memorable exercise, the aircraft developed engine trouble and the crew overshot the runway on landing. Nonetheless, this was valuable experience as they knew it would not be the last time they encountered problems during flights with the huge, heavy bombers.

On 10 April 1944 the crew left Syerston, posted to 467 Squadron, RAAF, which was based at RAF Waddington in Lincolnshire. For the majority Australian crew members, it must have been akin to a posting home.

Oscar's RAAF pennant displaying both his navigator and preferred observer brevets, and his flight sergeant crown insignia (author image).

CHAPTER 5

# A HEAVY WEAPON OF WAR: THE AVRO LANCASTER

The Avro Lancaster was a four-engine heavy bomber designed and built for the RAF by the Avro engineering company. Sturdy, rugged and reliable, it quickly became the Bomber Command workhorse. The Lancaster was designed with a long, continuous bomb bay which could carry the largest bombs used by the RAF, its payloads often reaching up to 18,000lbs in weight. It could also carry smaller bombs and incendiaries in addition to its primary payload. While designed as a night bomber, it performed well in other roles, including daylight precision bombing. The Lancaster was also a pilot's aircraft, a joy to fly with none of the handling idiosyncrasies common to other aircraft of the period. According to Sir Arthur 'Bomber' Harris, the Lancaster was the aircraft that made the escalation of the night bomber offensive over Germany possible, Harris adding that it was the 'greatest single factor in winning the war'.[21] Some 7374 Lancasters were produced, with 3932 aircraft lost on operations. This figure represents over 20,000 aircrew killed, wounded or captured. Only two of the 17 Lancasters that survive today are airworthy.

The bomb aimer did double duty as the front gunner in the Lancaster, where he would stand with his feet in much the same position for both roles. The left front corner of the front escape hatch hole is visible along the bottom edge of the picture (below) underneath the green seat.

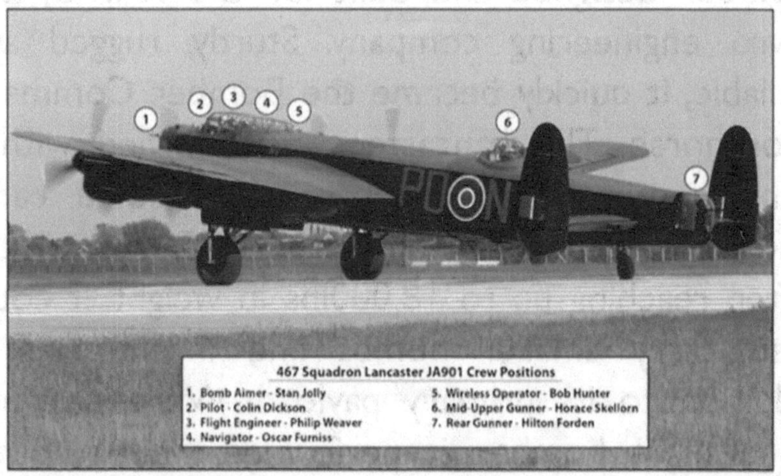


Lancaster III PA474 pictured at RAF Waddington. The 467 Squadron codes and the crew positions on Oscar Furniss' aircraft, 'Naughty Nan', have been overlaid in this image (original image Howard Heeley, graphic by Angela Elliott).

The bomb aimer's workplace—where he lay on his stomach (author image).

The cockpit of Lancaster 'Just Jane': the pilot sat on the left, the flight engineer or second pilot on the right. Access to the front gunner/bomb aimer compartment is beneath the right-hand controls (Lincolnshire Aviation Heritage Centre image).

The navigator's desk, with its maps, simple plotting implements and flight calculators. Overhead and to his right are some of the first-generation electronic navigation aids. The myriad of instruments provides some indication of why it took two years to train a navigator.

The H2S navigation system developed during the war (author images).

Navigator Phil Massey describes a trip home from a bombing raid on Kiel in northern Germany, the aircraft flying through a storm of flak:

> I was just wondering how the hell we had got away alive when Street [the pilot] yelled in a muffled voice, 'Navigator, I've been hit!' I nearly died! I could imagine myself collecting the DFM [Distinguished Flying Medal] for flying the kite back to England! We could all hear old Street panting and blowing over the intercom, so I asked him if he wanted me to come and take over. He said he thought that he would be alright though he couldn't feel his left hand at all.

I worked out a safe course for us to steer and told him I'd come and patch his hand as soon as he thought it wise for me to stop watching for fighters. They were near us all the time. Then, after a while, he called again and said he thought his hand was OK. The glove was cut open and his hand was scratched but the shock had numbed the whole of his arm. As soon as we were in comparative safety I went up behind him, dropped his armour plating and gave him some hot coffee. He'd got a bit of frostbite! I was sweating cobs![22]

Wireless operator and navigator in situ (AWM UK2052).

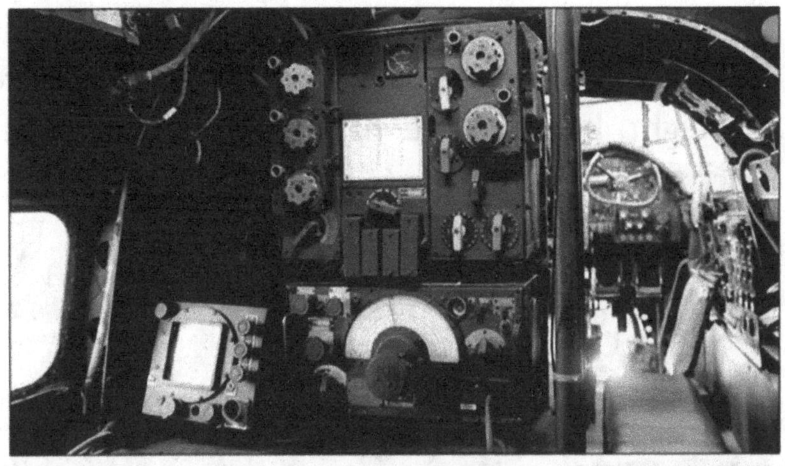

Wireless operator's radios and flight engineer's panel forward on the right (author image).

Wireless operator Bill Wareham, who also flew for 467 Squadron, described his actions once his aircraft took off on a night raid:

> I would now get back down into my seat, switch my gear on and check that everything was working all right. This in itself [provided] a sense of satisfaction. Everybody would call up each other and make sure we were all in touch. Of course, I only had to look round the corner to see the navigator. We'd then go off, come back and then set course. We would have gained about 8000 feet. We would be climbing all the time, at about 155 airspeed. We used to try and get up to about 20,000 feet, which we usually managed. Thus we were away from the light flak. By the time we

got to the Dutch coast, if we were going that way, we would be at our desired height, because we had a good aircraft.[23]

The flight engineer's second set of instruments, on the right side of the aircraft behind the second pilot's seat (author image).

At the time he was using these instruments, the flight engineer would face to the right, his right shoulder pushed up next to the navigator's right shoulder.

Moving around inside a Lancaster bomber was never easy because of the centre spar. The spar gave the aircraft great strength and load-carrying capacity but prevented the modification of the bomb bay to take larger bombs.

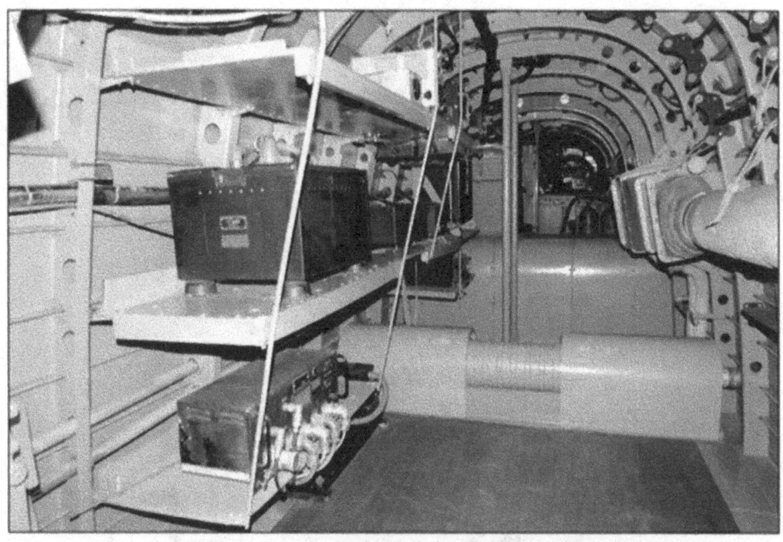

Centre of a Lancaster without the lower section of the mid-upper gunner's turret fitted (author image).

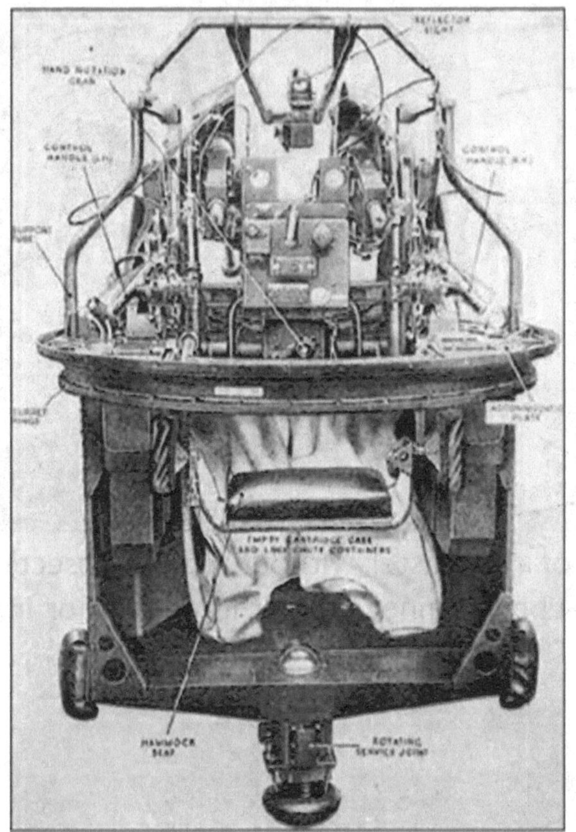

The mid-upper gun turret with the seat suspended on a leather strap (R. Wallace Clarke, British Aircraft Armament, Vol. I, RAF Gun Turrets from 1914 to the Present Day, Patrick Stephens Ltd., United Kingdom, 1993).

The rollers under the gun barrels followed a profiled track to lift the barrels so the trajectory of the rounds passed over tail fins and propellers (author image).

The mid-upper gunner was as restricted in his movements as the rear gunner. He stowed his parachute high on the right side and then climbed into his turret via a step on the left side. This was by no means simple; he had to step over the ammunition tracks for the rear gun turret plus an assortment of fire extinguishers and other equipment. He then threaded himself over the floor of the turret and up behind the back ends of the two Browning .303 machine-guns. He sat on a leather stirrup which he clipped up under himself once in position. He effectively sat in a playground-style swing for the duration of the flight.

The 360° field of view of the mid-upper gunner gave him the best view in the aircraft and he was regarded as the pilot's second set of eyes. The lower half of the turret resembled half a tin can sectioned vertically. The two guns had a roller under each barrel which followed a profiled track fixed to the fuselage around the turret lip. This cam track lifted the guns to prevent the rounds striking the tail fins or propellers. This sometimes made tracking and firing at an enemy aircraft difficult as the enemy would be firmly in the sights of the guns until the tail fins or propellers came into the line of fire and the opportunity was lost.

The turret sits on the track under the bubble and the lower section protrudes into the fuselage taking half the headroom (Wallace Clarke, British Aircraft Armament, Vol. I).

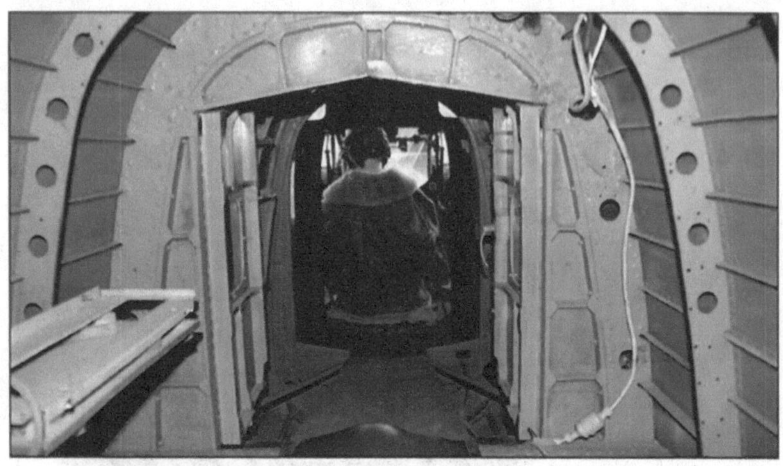

View from the mid-upper gunner position adjacent to the rear door. The gunner accessed the turret by moving feet first along the passageway (author image).

The rear gunner was the pilot's third set of eyes. However his was the most vulnerable position and the most difficult to access. The gunner sat in his turret without his parachute (there was no room) having closed the doors to allow the turret to rotate. Rear gunners often wore only heated slippers because there was no room for their boots. One of their escape options was to turn the turret to full lock and fall out backwards, hopefully once they had retrieved their parachute.

If the hydraulic lines providing power to the rear turret were damaged, as they were when Oscar's Lancaster was attacked, the gunner had nowhere to go. Bob Hunter noted as he peered through the fire and smoke that the rear turret was pointing straight back. The turret could not have rotated because the hydraulic lines were severed and the oil was fuelling the mid-section fire.

Many gunners removed the Perspex between the two guns as this gave them much better vision—but also increased exposure to hypothermia (author image).

The Lancaster was fitted with a Rolls Royce Merlin engine. This extraordinary engine was designed by Britain's foremost engineering works to counter some of the extremely advanced engines being fitted to German fighters. The Merlin engine was first trialled in 1933 and was known as the PV-12. Another three years of development followed in which the engine was operated at full capacity to ascertain its breakdown point. It finally entered production in 1936.

The Merlin engine is a liquid-cooled V12 cylinder configuration of 27 litres (1650 cubic inches), in which a single overhead cam shaft per bank operates four valves per cylinder. The engine was supercharged. The initial power target was 1000 horsepower (hp) and this was improved to around 1300hp for most operational aircraft. Final developments pushed power to 1650hp for normal and to 2640hp for special applications. Most of the performance enhancements were the result of improved supercharger technology and better quality fuel.

A Rolls Royce Merlin engine with shorter DC6 propeller blades operating at 2300 rpm at RAF Hendon (author image).

Most installations of the Merlin engine have the exhaust pods angled rearward as either six individual ports or three paired ports each side of the engine. The volume of exhaust gas being produced at 300mph (500kph) was equivalent to 70lbs' thrust, or around 70hp. The extra thrust was sufficient to increase the top speed of a Spitfire in level flight by 10mph to 360mph (600kph).

A Mk VIII Spitfire with a Rolls Royce Merlin engine, rear-pointing exhaust flanges and a four-blade propeller (author image).

The Merlin engine was also built under licence in the US by Packard USA. Total engine production reached almost 150,000 units, with each engine costing around £2000 to produce. The Rolls Royce-manufactured engines were primarily used in Spitfires, Hurricanes and Mosquitos while the Lancaster and the P51 Mustang were generally fitted with Packard engines.

The first prototypes of the German Messerschmitt Bf 109 fighter produced in 1935 were fitted with Rolls Royce Kestrel engines, a non-supercharged predecessor of the Merlin. The last Bf 109s, built after World War II for the Spanish Air Force, were fitted with Rolls Royce Merlin engines. The engine was later developed in non-supercharged form as the Meteor and was used in the British-built Centurion tank which served the Australian Army in Korea, Malaya and Vietnam.

The de Havilland Mosquito used by the Pathfinder squadrons was powered by two Rolls Royce Merlin engines similar to those in the Lancaster and Spitfire, and could carry a 4000lb bomb load. It was a fascinating aircraft, made predominantly of timber—balsa, plywood and spruce—and engaged the skills of the many carpenters who were under-utilised as Britain geared up for war. It was proposed by de Havilland in 1938 as a swift, light, two-seater bomber carrying no armaments and using speed as its main weapon. The Mosquito was small and fast—the fastest in the RAF—and, as it was non-metallic, it flew under the German radar with a significantly diminished chance of detection. Employed as a pathfinder, it would drop coloured flares on a target as a reference point for the heavy bombers.

The de Havilland Mosquito (de Havilland Aircraft Museum Trust collection).

The Mosquitos of the Pathfinder squadrons played a vital role in bomber missions over Europe and those operating with 467 Squadron were no exception. The Pathfinders were to have a significant influence on the events of the raid on Mailly-le-Camp in May 1944.

## CHAPTER 6

# OSCAR'S NEW HOME, 467 SQUADRON, RAAF, AND 'NAUGHTY NAN'

The 467 Squadron badge and motto: recidite adversarius atque ferociter ('retreat, enemy and fiercely', loosely translated as 'Your opponents will retreat because of your courageous attack').

No.467 Squadron was formed at RAF Scampton, Lincolnshire, on 7 November 1942 and equipped with Avro Lancaster heavy bombers. Under the terms of the Empire Air

Training Scheme, the squadron was nominally a RAAF unit, but was manned by a mixture of Commonwealth personnel, the majority initially British. As the war progressed however, increasing numbers of Australians joined the unit. The squadron was an element of No.5 Group, RAF Bomber Command, and flew its first operation on 2 January 1943. It was then transferred to RAF Bottesford, Leicestershire, for a year before returning to Lincolnshire, settling at RAF Waddington until the end of hostilities.

Unusually, the squadron was initially formed with three flights of six aircraft rather than the customary two flights, and its flights were designated A, B and C. However it lost its third flight in November 1943 when this was used to raise 463 Squadron, RAAF, another heavy bomber unit flying Lancaster bombers. Squadron records indicate that there were generally 19 or 20 aircraft on strength at 467 throughout April-May 1944. On its first operational night from its new base at RAF Waddington on 18 November 1943, the CO noted that the squadron put 25 bombers in the air. Colin Dickson and his crew were allocated a nine-month-old Lancaster III, JA901, PO-N, affectionately known as 'Naughty Nan'. PO is the identification code and radio call sign for 467 Squadron and the last letter, N, is the squadron identifier for the aircraft, effectively its registration number. JA901 is the bomber's production number.

Pilot Officer Colin Dickson in a photo taken at around 8.00 pm on the evening of 3 May 1944, just after Colin received news of his commissioning to pilot officer (Jolly family image).

The symbols on the left flank of an aircraft under the pilot's window indicated the number of missions the aircraft had flown and identified the pilot of each mission. Each pilot had his preferred symbol. The markings on the side of Nan in this image were those used by the previous pilot and had not been updated.

Nan's 10th mission, marked at the end of the top row, almost ended in disaster when she landed in North Africa and was considered 'written off'. Nan's 15th mission, marked at the end of the second row, was her last in 1943. In the photograph above, Nan was about to take off on her 38th (and final) mission. Colin Dickson was one of 12 pilots to fly this aircraft.

Naughty Nan—JA901—was one of 550 Lancasters ordered from A.V. Roe in Chadderton in late 1941 and delivered as Mark III Lancasters between June and December 1943. As an early production aircraft of this contract, the bomber had been fitted with Packard Merlin 28 engines. On 14 August 1943, JA901 took off for a mission bombing Milan, Italy, piloted by Flying Officer W.D. Marshall. The mission was to end unexpectedly as the post-operation intelligence report revealed some weeks later:

> Bombing – MILAN – sortie completed. Bombed centre of two green TIs [target indicators] from 12500 at 0132 ... Fires burning well. Attack on FIAT factory also appeared to be going strong. Set course late [from Bottesford] and ran late the whole way. Encountered flak near Le Havre and soon after attacked by fighter. Port outer feathered due to lack of oil pressure. Crossed ALPS 15500–15000ft, losing height. Jettisoned 4 SBC [small bomb containers] over ALPS to maintain height. Remaining three engines not running well. Unable to maintain height and sank to 9000ft flying at

> 145mph ... Six attacks by fighters and made off for AFRICA. Home to BISKRA ... and landed on a small flare path.

Biskra Airfield in Algeria was the major base of the US Twelfth Air Force during the North Africa campaign. The base was substantial and would certainly have had the capacity to handle a four-engine bomber such as a Lancaster. The small bomb containers referred to in the report could carry 236 of the 4lb bombs or 24 of the 30lb bombs, and these were often jettisoned to reduce weight.

The CO of 467 Squadron noted the incident in his operations log comments for 15 August 1943, initially expressing some alarm:

> Quite a shock this morning as F/O Marshall failed to return and casualty signals had been made out (but not dispatched) before word came through that he was OK and had landed in North Africa. His plane was written off but all the crew were safe thank goodness.

The general procedure for reclaiming damaged aircraft within the UK was to remove the wings and transport the lot by lorry back to Avro either for repair, reconstruction or scrap. Aircraft outside the UK were considered too expensive to retrieve.

Jack Colpus' aircrew and Naughty Nan's ground crew in snow at Waddington, January 1944. Jack Colpus is walking beneath the ladder (Colpus family image).

While JA901 was extensively damaged, she was clearly not considered beyond repair. The aircraft had evidently suffered multiple attacks by fighters, but the reports on her condition make no mention of major control damage to the aircraft. Such damage would also have prevented her pilot landing safely. The main problem lay with the engines, one of which had failed completely, while the other three were performing sporadically at best. The large number of holes in the body had also undoubtedly made it difficult for the pilot to hold altitude.

Bomber Command was already flying missions over southern Europe, many of its aircraft then flying on to North Africa. With the collapse of Axis forces in North Africa in May 1943, the RAF had gained access to over 200 landing grounds in the region and, by implication, also had a servicing capacity for its aircraft while on the ground. Here the crew rested and the bombers were refuelled and re-armed. The following night the bombers flew back over another target and home to England. During her three-month unscheduled stopover at the US Twelfth Air Force's Biskra Airfield, JA901 was repaired to an airworthy standard before being flown back to the UK where she immediately returned to operational tasking. It was only later that her ground crew discovered that she had been fitted with a Rolls Royce Merlin engine taken from a Spitfire rather than a Packard Merlin. She had flown home with one fighter and three bomber engines.

In 38 missions JA901 flew to Germany 30 times, France five times and Italy three times. She flew 13 missions to Berlin and was flown by Flight Lieutenant Jack Colpus, DFC, on 13 occasions. Pilot Officer Colin Dickson flew her on operations just three times. In terms of performance, she was regarded as unreliable, a label justified by the fact that she returned from around half of her missions with a mechanical issue of some description. On no fewer than four occasions she failed to return to the 467 Squadron base due to mechanical problems. Her mission history (included as Appendix 4) is telling and clearly indicates that her reputation for unreliability was well deserved.

In late April 1944, JA901 suffered engine failure in one of her starboard engines and was under repair until 1 May when she was tested for airworthiness. She was declared unfit for tasking and her crew transferred to L-Love, which had no bomb cameras. JA901 completed another test flight on the morning of 3 May 1944 and was considered airworthy for her next mission. It would prove to be her last.

# CHAPTER 7

# SERVING IN 467 SQUADRON

RAF Waddington sits nine kilometres south of the city of Lincoln in Lincolnshire, in the eastern part of the English Midlands. The station has a rich flying history, dating from the time of the Royal Flying Corps in 1916. While it closed for a few years following the end of World War I, it reopened as a bomber base in 1937. By the time it became home to 463 and 467 squadrons it was a well-appointed RAF station with brick and mortar buildings, a significant improvement on RAF Winthorpe.

The Sergeants' Mess at RAF Waddington, built in 1944, is typical of the standard of facilities on the base at the time (author image).

Oscar and his crew arrived at RAF Waddington on 10 April 1944 and took to the air almost immediately. In line with the practice of introducing new pilots to the real world of operations on their first night, Colin Dickson flew as second pilot with Flying Officer Gibbs in another aircraft, taking part in a raid on Tours in France, eager to gain experience before his first mission. While briefings for that mission were held, the remainder of Colin's crew packed 'window', the shredded aluminium strips used to jam German radar, into the other aircraft scheduled for the operation. 'Window' was generally stowed at the front of the aircraft so that the front gunner or bomb aimer could push it out through special chutes. A total of 18 aircraft—the entire squadron of three flights, each of six aircraft—were scheduled to attack the railway marshalling yards at Tours, just one element of a massive raid involving 789 aircraft. JA901—'Naughty Nan'—was flown by Flight Lieutenant Jack Colpus for the last time on the mission to Tours. Nineteen aircraft were lost, none from 467 Squadron.

The next day Oscar and the crew flew a daytime test flight while Colin Dickson flew once again as second pilot, this time on an operation to Aachen in Germany. In another massive raid, this time comprising 352 bombers, the town of

Aachen was extensively damaged, with fires devastating its central and southern suburbs. This was the most destructive attack on Aachen of the war. Nine aircraft were lost although, again, all the 467 Squadron aircraft returned safely.

On 12 April the crew flew daytime circuits, conducted bombing practice and completed exercises in fighter familiarisation which involved being attacked by a 'fighter' while the pilot's response was filmed for later analysis. The arrival of two new crews was greeted with relief as it meant that existing crews could be rotated, allowing men to be rested between operations. Prior to their arrival, every crew had been allocated an aircraft and flew on a daily basis. Now they were granted some well-deserved stand down.

By 14 April Oscar and his crew were flying Naughty Nan in daytime fighter familiarisation missions and also completing gunnery practice ready for their first mission, scheduled as a raid over Osnabrück. However bad weather forced the cancellation of the operation, but not before the crew had enjoyed the special dinner reserved for aircrews on operations—bacon and an egg. This was a particular treat as eggs were very scarce at the time. The mission was cancelled just as the crews were ready to start taxiing, with news of bad weather over the target. At this point the Merlin engines would have been running for at least 20 minutes as the crew conducted their pre-flight checks.

The next few days saw the crew complete more daytime cross-country flights in Naughty Nan and spend the rest of the day in 'make and mend' activities. They were also treated to a visit by Air Vice Marshal H.A. Wrigley, Air Officer Commanding RAAF Overseas Headquarters. Such visits provided a welcome morale boost and reassured the Australians that they had not been forgotten by those at home.

On 17 April the crew was scheduled for its first operation, a raid over Paris which was eventually cancelled, a decision greeted by howls of disappointment. However on 18 April they completed a scheduled daytime bombing practice in Naughty Nan and followed this with their first night operation—the rescheduled raid over Paris.

Having endured the frustration of two previous operations being cancelled prior to take-off, the crew must have been jubilant to finally have completed an operation in Naughty Nan. The target was the Juvisy railway yards on the southern outskirts of Paris and their takeoff time was 8.30 pm. They experienced the exhilaration of being farewelled by a large group of base personnel, assembled at the end of the runway to wave them off. Once over the target, they dropped 500lb bombs with six-hour delay fuses. These delay fuses exploded instantaneously if the bomb was disturbed by attempts to defuse it or move it to a safe area. A total of 14,000lbs of bombs were dropped at 11.35 pm. There was minimal flak and only a few aircraft were lost. The crew regarded this operation as a 'quiet trip', but successful in achieving its objective, and hoped fervently that it was a sign of what was to come.

In one of his dispatches on air operations, Air Marshal 'Bomber' Harris wrote of these raids:

> In most attacks the bombing accuracy was of a high, and in many, of an outstanding high order. For instance, at two important centres near Paris—Juvisy and La Chapelle—the whole railway complex was almost annihilated as a result of the single attacks, engine round-houses and depots, marshalling yards, rolling stock, and nearly all other facilities had almost entirely disappeared. Reconnaissance showed complete wildernesses resembling nothing so much as a telescope view of the extinct craters of the moon.[24]

This raid also marked the first time Naughty Nan's crew had experienced enemy fire. New pilots and crew reacted in various ways to the chatter of enemy machine-guns or the buffeting of flak. Pilot George Unwin from 19 Squadron, RAF, recalled his reaction the first time he encountered an enemy aircraft:

> The first time I was shot at, I froze. I saw a Messerschmitt coming up inside me and I saw little sparks coming from the front end of him. I knew he was shooting at me—and I did nothing. Absolutely nothing, I just sat there. I was frozen for ten or fifteen seconds. I just sat there and watched him shoot at me. He hit me, but just knocked a few holes in the back of my aircraft. From then on, I realised what a mug I'd been and never did it again. I suppose one isn't used to being shot at in any walk of life and if most people found somebody shooting at them, they would freeze.[25]

The men returned safely from their first sortie as a crew, Colin Dickson having completed his third mission. The next day Colin asked a confused Stan if he had followed the bombing instructions he had been given in the operational briefing. The bomb aimer's task was to direct the pilot to steer the aircraft so that he could align the bomb sights with the target indication flares. Stan looked bewildered, and Colin explained that there had been another Lancaster directly above them and he was concerned that

Stan had diverged from the course he had been given. Rear gunner Hilton Forden then interjected, remarking that he had only discovered the presence of the other aircraft as the bombs had rained past, just missing his turret.

It was not uncommon for an aircraft to be damaged by bombs from above. On 3 August 1944 a Lancaster on a mission to Trossy-Saint Maximin was bombed from above. The mid-upper gunner had just finished announcing that 'a Lanc above has just opened its bomb doors' when the crew felt two massive thumps and the aircraft shuddered. One 1000lb bomb had gone through the left wing just behind the inner engine and taken the undercarriage with it. It had missed the front and rear spars by inches. Another 1000lb bomb had clipped the outer end of the right wing. The pilot, Flying Officer Ryan, somehow brought his damaged aircraft home and belly-landed at Wittering. Miraculously, the crew emerged unhurt.

Oscar and his crew rested the next day, with many of the men venturing into Lincoln sightseeing. The following day Oscar's health broke down again and he returned to the sick quarters with bronchitis. By this stage 467 Squadron had more crew than aircraft so, with Oscar now admitted to the base hospital, the crew had an extended break and Naughty Nan was flown by another crew on a mission to attack the bomb marshalling yards at La Chapelle in France. The mission over La Chapelle was to end in sadness for Oscar and his crew as Colin Dickson's friend, Flying Officer Ken Feeney, and his crew in Y-Yoke were listed as missing, having failed to return from the sortie. Post-war reports suggested that the bomber had been hit by flak over the target and crashed at Le Blanc Mesnil on the south-eastern side of Paris-le-Bourget Airport, killing Feeney and his six crew members. At the time of his death, Feeney was aged just 27.

A photo of Pilot Officer Ken Feeney (back row, far right) with his crew and Lancaster Y-Yoke just prior to their fateful mission to La Chapelle (AWM P11713.003).

The next few days were spent, once again, in 'make and mend' while Oscar remained in the base hospital. His stay in hospital would extend until the end of April. One of the major parties he missed was Anzac Day which was recorded in the squadron log as a day of 'celebrations in the mess'. The party clearly marked the release of tension with the log entry: 'A real drunken do. 400 gallons of beer down the dusty lane.' Hangovers were not uncommon, particularly within the ranks of the fighter pilots. Curing them was often a matter of ingenuity, as Sergeant Charlton Haw of 504 Squadron, RAF, describes: 'If you had a bit of a hangover, you sat in your aircraft and put the oxygen full on and it worked like magic. It cleared your head straight away.' But life in the mess was not simply a matter of socialising. As one CO of 460 Squadron put it, 'The boys who get into scrapes in the pubs are the ones least likely to crack up.' Unwinding over a drink was regarded as a necessary coping mechanism. Oscar certainly released his inner tensions over a few drinks. In one of his diary entries Bob Hunter promised himself he would never buy Oscar another drink, noting that a drunk Oscar 'made more noise' than Bob's own father 'ever knew how to'.[26]

467 Squadron Lancaster I, R5868, S-Sugar, being loaded for its 97th operation on 23 April 1944. Note the large number of mission tokens below the pilot's window (somethingverybig.com image).

S-Sugar restored to its original condition and now on display at RAF Hendon, London, having completed 137 operations. Pilot Jack Colpus brought S-Sugar home from one mission with five feet of wing missing. This bomber also flew in the Mailly raid alongside Naughty Nan and Colin Dickson's crew (author image).

On 27 April Naughty Nan and her crew, minus Oscar and Jack Skellorn who were both ill, flew a night-time 'bull's eye' exercise towards Aachen, one of three aircraft to participate. The purpose of a bull's eye exercise varied. Occasionally it was an operational sortie, while at other times it was a navigation exercise usually conducted over safe territory such as Scotland. The sortie was not expected to attract enemy fire—although occasionally it did. The flight towards Aachen resembled an infantry reconnaissance patrol designed to probe the enemy's defences to determine their strengths and weaknesses. The pilot was likely to be caught by searchlights and could practise his skills in evading them.

The 467 Squadron log records that, on the night of 26/27 April 1944, JA901 was flown by Flight Sergeant Johns on a mission to Schweinfurt and shot down a fighter en route. This was to be Naughty Nan's last mission into Germany. Flight Lieutenant Jack Colpus' crew had been taken off the operation following an accident. The mid-upper gunner was testing his guns when his clothing fouled the mechanism and caused the guns to fire. The gunfire hit the rear turret and injured the rear gunner, who was struck in the eye by shards of Perspex. A later report stated that, following treatment, he was deemed 'quite serviceable', to use the RAF parlance of the day.

On 28 April, a night operation to Saint-Médard-en-Jalles (Bordeaux) was scheduled for Naughty Nan and her regular crew. However Oscar and Jack Skellorn both remained ill and other crew members replaced them for this trip. Ultimately the mission was aborted as the aircraft experienced engine trouble soon after takeoff. The starboard inner engine began overheating almost as soon as the course was set and caught fire. The engine was 'feathered' and the fire was soon extinguished, to the immense relief of the crew. However they were forced to jettison eight 1000lb general purpose and a 500lb medium capacity bomb over the English Channel given the considerable risk of the fire flaring again and igniting one of the bombs. Eventually the entire mission was aborted due to bad weather over the target.

'Feathering' a propeller or an engine is akin to putting a moving motor vehicle into neutral, turning the engine off and coasting. The flight engineer had four shrouded (capped) buttons on his control panel, one for each propeller.

Depressing one of these buttons immediately rotated the propeller blades parallel to the line of flight (the thin edge of the propeller would rotate to the front so there was no load against the blade) to take the load off the engine. The propeller was then hydraulically disengaged from its drive shaft and the engine was shut down. The engine was 'feathered' when the oil pressure dropped dangerously low, the engine temperature was perilously high or when there was a fire in the engine area. The most visible sign of a propeller which has been 'feathered' during flight is the drop in its revolutions—it turns idly while the others continue to spin normally. Beneath the shrouded buttons was a row of four red buttons which activated the engine bay fire extinguishers.

The shrouded buttons on the right are used to 'feather' the propellers. The red light in the centre of each button is the fire warning indicator. The four buttons below activate the engine bay fire extinguishers (Lincolnshire Aviation Heritage Centre image).

Following this aborted mission, Colin Dickson's crew pooled their poetic resources and composed this little ditty which became well known around Waddington. Much of the credit must go to Bob Hunter who was a prolific composer of such ditties:

We are the crew of Naughty Nan
and though we do the best we can
We always seem in trouble's way
with gremlins at their wicked play
the engines stop, electrics fail
we'd do much better with a sail
the turrets always seem to tire
of going round and never fire.
So it's out to The Wash and drop the load
to scare the fish in their abode
another target, failed to 'prang'
another bloody boomerang.

On 29 April the crew was finally back to full strength and flew a night operation over Bordeaux, the target once again the Saint-Médard-en-Jalles ammunition works. This was a successful mission, the bombs finding their target, and the explosion lighting up the sky as if daylight had assumed a reddened hue. The crew flew a different aircraft—DV373—on what was their longest flight to date, Naughty Nan out of action due to continuing repairs to the engine that had caught fire.

Servicing or replacing a V12 engine in a Lancaster is not a simple job Most servicing was done in the open air—rain, hail or snow (author image).

The operations log report for the crew's mission on 29 April 1944 reads:

> DV373 Sortie completed. Clear. Bombed 1 red spot fire from 5500' at 0228–3x1000lb GP, 5x1000lb GP (USA), 4x1000lb MC, 4x500lb MC. Fires burning in wood S of target possibly started by flares. Explosion on target 0226. Much concentrated bombing on red spot flares. Defences very light on whole route and target area. Heard nothing

of leaders, only some French—everything else O.K.

The CO's report for the same mission records:

> Another good day with all back once again, and the crews certainly enjoyed the trip. The weather was hazy but this time the target was well marked and all crews had to hold onto their hats for the tremendous explosion was throwing aircraft around. All members of [Squadron Leader] Smith's crew met the top of the aircraft with their heads. Aircraft flying at 4000 would have been destroyed as they bombed because they would be low enough to be exposed to the shock waves from the exploding ordinance. According to all reports the explosions were easily heard above the engine drone. Considered to be a very successful effort.

By 1 May 1944 daylight test flights of Naughty Nan indicated that she remained unfit for tasking. The crew completed a night operation to Toulouse in another bomber, the target the aircraft factory. With the last-minute change of aircraft, Colin Dickson had no camera installed and was unable to secure an aiming point. Three of the other crews also experienced difficulty in securing aiming points. Nonetheless the mission was declared a success with smoke seen coming from the target.

Operations into France were regarded as 'easy', with little opposition. This fitted the RAF rating of a mission to France as equating to a third of a mission to Germany. Indeed, as recently as March 1944, Bomber Command had confirmed that missions to Scandinavia, Holland, Belgium and France were not deemed as dangerous as a mission to Germany. Ratings were important as mission numbers were tallied towards the 30 missions required by aircrew to complete a tour of duty and fulfil their service obligation. Irrespective, the average life of aircrew was 10 missions while that of the aircraft was 30. Following the disastrous Mailly raid in May 1944, this policy was amended so that all missions were rated of equal service obligation value.

On 3 May a daytime test flight of Naughty Nan was completed to confirm her operational air worthiness. The flight was successful and she was declared ready for the next mission which was scheduled for that night. This vote of confidence in Naughty Nan may not have been shared by her crew who already considered her very unreliable. They were not alone. Jack Colpus' crew had reached the same conclusion having flown 13 missions in the bomber. However this was perhaps the thought furthest from their minds as they prepared for their mission—their first as a complete crew in Naughty Nan for two weeks. It would also be their last.

# CHAPTER 8

# PREPARING FOR THE FINAL MISSION

At 4.00 pm on 3 May 1944, Wing Commander Arthur Doubleday commenced his briefing to the 10 crews from 467 Squadron scheduled for the night's mission. His first action was to uncover a map of France on the wall to reveal a line of red wool stretching from Waddington, south to Beachy Head, turning east to a point just below Reims, and finally south-east to a red-headed pin which pierced a point alongside the village of Mailly-le-Camp. Mailly-le-Camp sat adjacent to a series of French Army barracks, built on the eastern edge of the village in 1902.

The Mailly-le-Camp barracks before the raid of May 1944 (delcampe.net image).

British intelligence had received word from the French Resistance that the German *21st Panzer Division* had moved into the camp, clearly on its way to the channel coast. This was less than five weeks prior to Operation Overload—the D Day landings at Normandy—and, while the Germans were aware that the Allies were planning a major operation, they had no idea what it would involve or where it would take place. The British were working hard to persuade the Germans that the operation would comprise an amphibious attack launched from Dover towards Calais—the point at which the English Channel is just 40 kilometres wide.

Reconnaissance image of Mailly-le-Camp barracks taken on 23 April 1944 (image courtesy of the Mailly Association).

Wing Commander Doubleday described the route to the listening aircrew as a series of waypoints from Waddington to a prescribed point north of Paris with a turning point to the target south of Reims. The route home was likewise a series of waypoints designed to guide the aircraft to the French coast, then home to Waddington. The Pathfinders, which flew ahead of a bombing raid to mark the target for the bombers, would use red flares to distinguish them from flares frequently lit by the Germans to divert the bombers. The forecast was good and promised fine weather with just a few scattered clouds and a full moon. Doubleday cautioned the crews to watch carefully for German night fighters.

Night fighters posed a constant threat. Jack Colpus described a close shave with a night fighter during a raid over Germany:

> ...we experienced a near head-on collision with a German ME 110 night fighter who obviously thought he was approaching from our rear. With a closing speed of 600mph [1000kph] it was all over in a flash—I froze as he whizzed overhead. He was expecting to see me but I wasn't expecting to see him. He was probably using a radar device to intercept us at the time.[27]

It was the responsibility of the two turret gunners to keep a sharp lookout for night fighters. They would be kept busy during the Mailly raid, the area notoriously populated with numerous *Luftwaffe* fighter bases.

Because of the high toll of French civilian casualties as a consequence of past raids, the bombing heights above ground level were lowered to between 5000 and 8000 feet. The first aircraft on target would bomb from the lowest altitude so that they were not flying through the bombs of the aircraft above them. Bombing altitudes were progressively staggered up to 8000 feet. Naughty Nan would be in the first and lowest wave of bombers at 5000 feet. The crew were justifiably concerned about being bombed from above given their earlier close shave during the raid on Bordeaux.

The primary target was the German *21st Panzer Division,* which occupied a compact section of the barracks.

Men from the 21st Panzer Division load their tanks on trains at Mailly for movement to the English Channel the day the bombers were preparing for the mission (Bundesarchiv image).

On 3 May 1944 Bomber Command allocated 352 aircraft to a raid designed to destroy the *21st Panzer Division.* Among them were the 10 aircraft of 467 Squadron, including Naughty Nan and her crew who now began the lengthy process of preparing for a night operation.

Aircrew donned standard flying apparel for each mission which included two pairs of long underwear, with one pair often electrically heated. Electrically heated slippers were also often worn, although not on this mission as the crew were flying at a lower altitude. The men pulled on battle jacket and trousers and a navy polo-neck sweater before adding a lambswool-lined flying jacket. A week earlier Colin Dickson's crew had also been issued new flying boots known as 'escape boots'. The bottom section of the boot was styled as a standard lace-up shoe while the canvas legging section was stitched to the sole and included a small knife. The knife was used to cut off the leggings so that the shoes appeared to be normal black dress shoes. Each crew member also had an individual parachute, parachute harness and Mae West flotation vest.

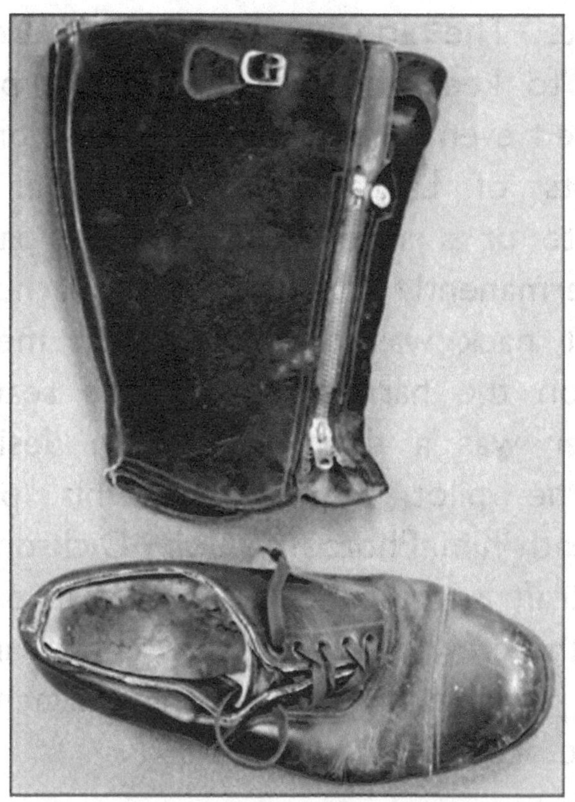

The new escape boot with the shoe section detached from its gaiter (author image).

There were three types of parachute available for aircrew, the choice of parachute generally dictated by the type of aircraft and the role of the crewman. The parachutes could be worn on the backside, back or belly. There were two variations of the backside/seat parachute.

The parachute harness was a common style for all parachutes, a double-thickness white cotton and linen mixture webbing which was sewn together with attachment points to suit the parachute. The attachment hooks were strong enough to keep the airman and the parachute connected even when reduced to just one hook.

Pilots of Lancasters wore either a seat parachute or a seat pack. The seat parachutes were permanently attached to the harness while the seat pack was clipped to two metal snap hooks on the harness. The pilot's seat in the Lancaster was a deep metal dish designed to allow the pilot to sit with his parachute underneath him. Photos of Colin Dickson outside the aircraft suggest he wore a seat pack. The rest of the crew members wore chest parachutes. These parachutes were easily attached and detached.

The standard parachute harness with the two quick release clips for parachute attachment fitted over the Mae West flotation device (author image).

The crews normally flew with their parachutes hanging on hooks close to their station in the aircraft as the chest-type parachutes in particular would have impeded the ability of the crewman to perform his routine tasks during the flight. Their stowage also allowed the men to move more freely around the aircraft. This was certainly the case for the rear and mid-upper gunners as there was insufficient space in the respective turrets for both the gunner and his parachute. In both cases the gunners' parachutes were held on a hook just outside the turret and the gunner would grab the parachute and clip it on when required. If the rear gunner discovered that he was unable to move forward because of fire or damage, he could rotate the turret to full lock and tip backwards out of it. This was the theory and, occasionally, it worked.

The airmen were also issued a survival kit which consisted of glucose tablets, barley sugar, chocolate, a short-handled shaver, a one-inch stick of shaving soap, 30 feet of fishing line, a hook and a sinker. Other items included cash—2000 French francs (approximately £10)—and a four-language card in French, Dutch, German and Spanish, two handkerchief-sized silk maps (the countries covered varied according to the mission and were usually a combination of France, Belgium and Holland or France and Spain), a tiny compass just 5/8 inch (15 millimetres) in diameter, often fashioned to resemble a button, and at least one passport-sized photograph of the airman wearing a civilian coat and tie to enable false identification papers to be made. Bob Hunter wrote later that, having been issued this kit, the crew now began to feel truly in the grip of the war.

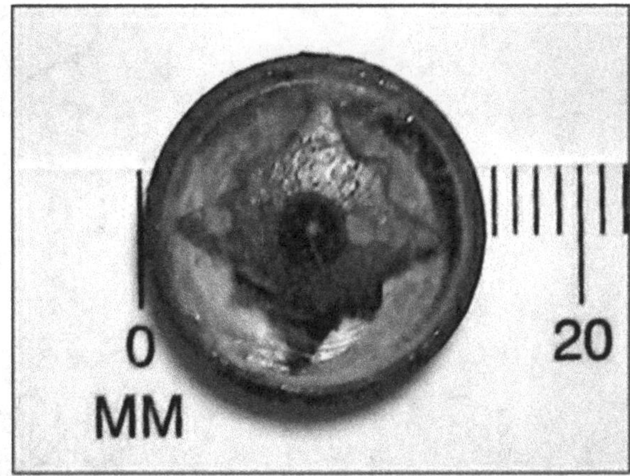


The evader button compass, just 15 millimetres in diameter. North, to the right, is still correct after 75 years (author image).

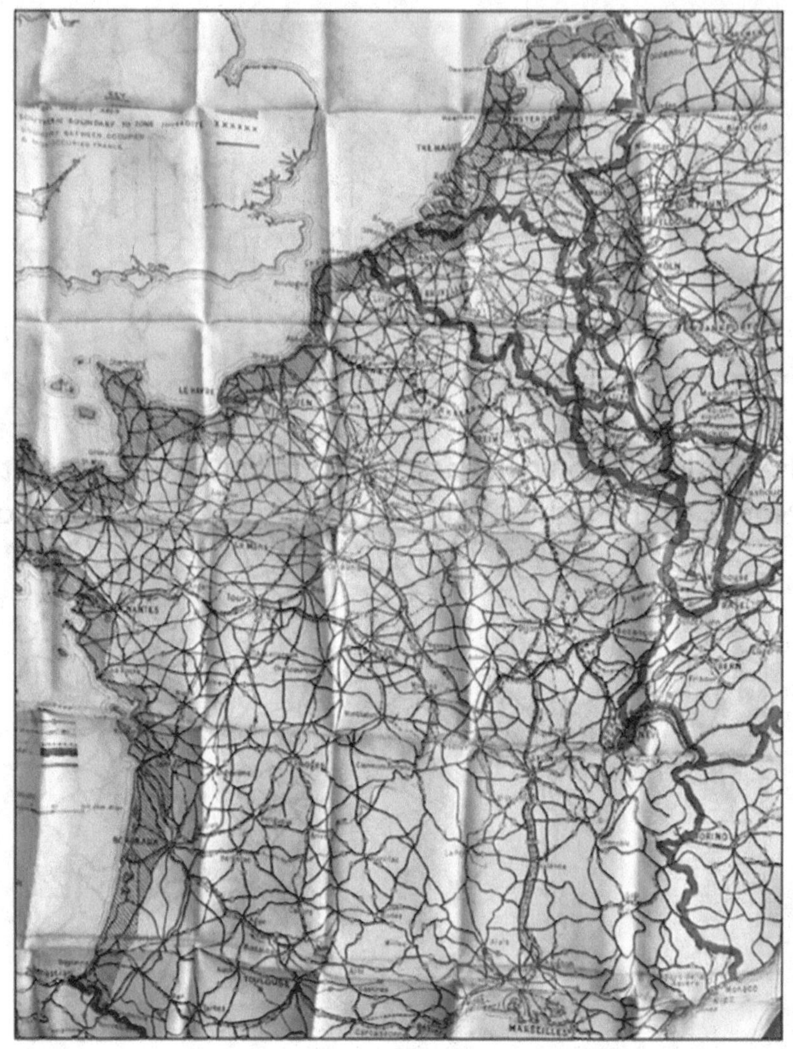
LE HAVRE
NANTES
TORINO
TOULOUSE
MARSEILLES

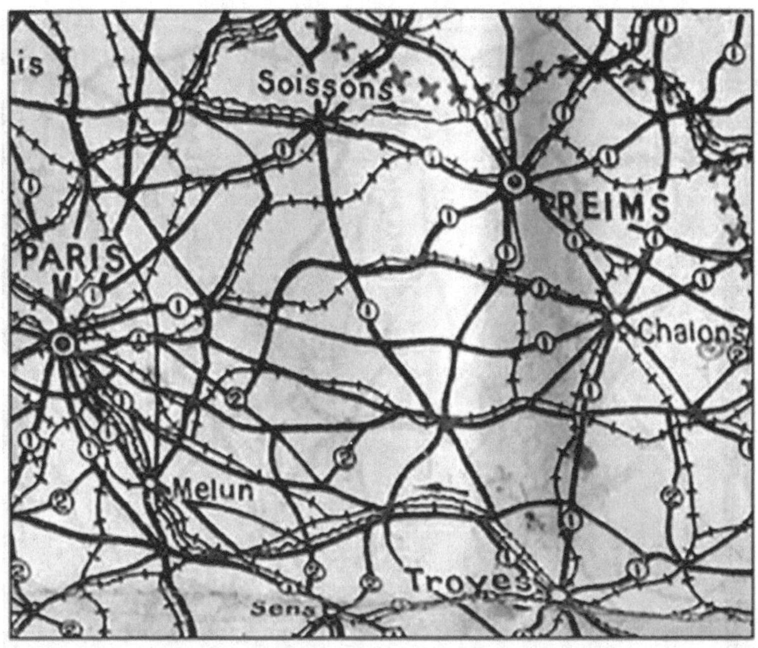


Stan Jolly's evader kit silk map of France, plus a zoom to the target area between Chalon and Troyes, and the envelope containing his four-language translation card (Jolly family images).

Bob was also struck by the fact that the crew would be bombing a German Panzer division in a French military camp from 5000 feet, their lowest altitude yet. He wondered whether, at that altitude, they would be able to 'see the buggers run'.[28] He may also have wondered just how clearly 'the buggers', their anti-aircraft defences and night fighters would be able to see him.

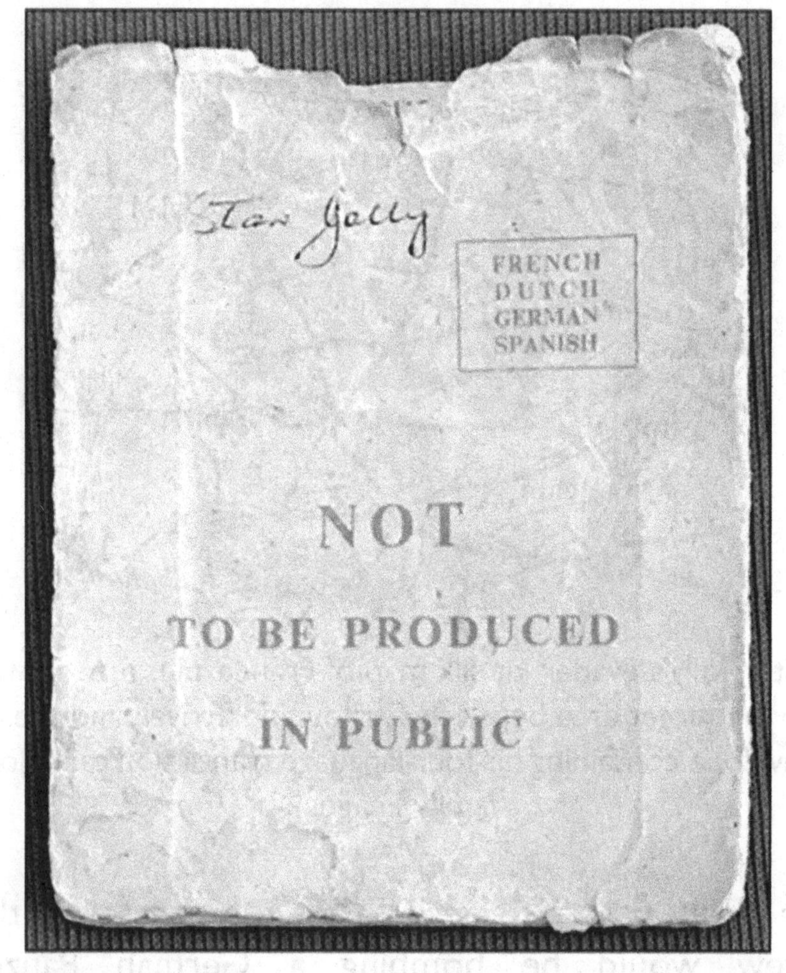
FRENCH
DUTCH
GERMAN
SPANISH
NOT
TO BE PRODUCED
IN PUBLIC

# CHAPTER 9

# THE OPERATION

Oscar attended the obligatory last-minute navigators' briefing as the vans backed up outside to take the crews to their aircraft across the dispersal area. The navigators' briefing would inform them of any corrections to the information they had received at lunchtime such as wind strength and direction en route and over the target. This information would assist them in their navigation calculations which routinely allowed for wind drift. Following the call to 'synchronise watches' which followed the final briefing, they too were loaded into the waiting vans. Every crew member was at his post in his aircraft 30 minutes prior to take-off to warm the engines and check the instruments. Having been delivered to their aircraft by the WAAF drivers, the crew stood around smoking their last cigarettes and making their farewells before climbing into the aircraft.

Aircraft JA901 PO-N—Naughty Nan—took off from Waddington at 9.49 pm on 3 May 1944, her mission to bomb the barracks adjacent to Mailly-le-Camp, two hours and 15 minutes away in German-occupied France. Colin Dickson was at the controls, buoyed by the fact that he had just been commissioned, his promotion from flight sergeant to pilot officer announced during the briefing. Colin had posed with his aircraft for a photograph and the crew enjoyed the morale boost provided by their popular pilot's promotion. Stan Jolly, front gunner and bomb aimer, sat in the nose of the aircraft, level with Colin Dickson's feet. Colin himself was strapped into the left-hand seat in the cockpit, sitting on his parachute. Philip (Taffy) Weaver, the flight engineer, stood on Colin's right, habitually standing in preference to sitting. The flight engineer had a second set of instruments that displayed engine revs, fuel levels, oil pressures and temperatures, as well as water temperatures in the four Packard Merlin engines mounted on the right side of the Lancaster behind where he stood. Seated behind the pilot, facing across the aircraft to the left-hand side in his blacked-out cubicle was navigator Oscar Furniss.

Radio operator Bob Hunter sat behind the navigator's position but facing forward at the controls of his wireless sets and Morse key. Like Oscar, Bob could not see what was happening outside the aircraft as his area was also curtained off to allow him to illuminate his desk without betraying the bomber's position. Between the wireless operator and the mid-upper gunner was a draught barrier. This partition prevented wind coming through the apertures in the front turret, funnelling through the aircraft and interfering with its performance. It also acted as a fire door and had an axe bolted to it. Horace 'Jack' Skellorn was suspended in the mid-upper gunner's turret and Hilton Forden was secure in his rear gunner's turret, both completing a final check of their guns, ammunition feed and heaters.

Naughty Nan was queued on the runway at RAF Waddington with a 12000lb bomb load in her belly (comprising one 4000lb and sixteen 500lb bombs) and 1600 gallons of 100 octane fuel in the tanks in her wings. Despite the fact that it was almost 10.00 pm, the two hours of daylight saving meant that it was still light outside. Each member of the crew now focused on the tasks specific to his position as the aircraft hummed in readiness. Colin, his hands firmly on the flight controls, watched the taxiways and runway for other aircraft while waiting for permission to take off, signalled by red and green lanterns, a measure designed to prevent the Germans intercepting radio instructions which would indicate the size of the bomber force. Navigator Oscar called the speed at regular intervals, relieving Colin of the necessity to monitor every instrument. Nan was the third aircraft off, her take-off speed under full load

115mph (185kph). Stan Jolly wrote later that Nan struggled to become airborne under the enormous weight of her payload. Flight Engineer Taffy, controlling engine power, revs and speed, provided maximum power to the aircraft, boosting the engine power to around 5400hp to lift the 30-tonne bomber into the air. Taffy's role was also designed to relieve the pilot's considerable burden, the flight engineer monitoring vital instruments on the pilot's behalf. Likewise, Stan had a double role, acting as Oscar's eyes for navigation points such as significant towns, coastlines, railways and church spires that Oscar was unable to see from his blacked-out cubicle.

From Waddington, Nan took off to the west and climbed to 10,000 feet before banking to the left and heading south towards Beachy Head, the southernmost point of the Sussex coast, just west of Eastbourne. The RAF had established a forward radar station at Beachy Head to improve communications with aircraft and this proved an excellent navigation point. Darkness had closed in by the time Nan flew to the west of Peterborough and, around an hour after take-off, she flew over Beachy Head, 150 miles (250 kilometres) south of Waddington and her final point on the English coast. The route across the English Channel was 70 miles (115 kilometres) and Nan's arrival over the French coast was greeted by Stan's announcement to Oscar: 'enemy coast ahead', the standard expression and his duty task as they flew over the French coast. This was their first navigation turning point.

Beachy Head—the crew's last view of England (author image).

Like any aeroplane flight there were long periods of tedium between take-off and the next scheduled activity. Banter among the crew was a common means of breaking up these periods as wartime pilot Jack Currie describes in his 1995 book on the Mailly raid, *Battle Under the Moon:*

> 'I am the captain of the aircraft', the pilot might remark, 'and I make the decisions.'

> 'Come off it,' the navigator would respond, 'you're just the driver. You wouldn't know which way to turn if I didn't tell you!'[29]

The sky lit up with searchlights on the left-hand side as they flew past Abbeville in northern France. Then a ball of fire to their right told the story of a fellow aircraft that would not reach the target, having been picked off by a night fighter. An enormous explosion signalled its death as it hit the ground and 12000lbs of ordinance and 1600 gallons of fuel ignited in a blazing finale.

Naughty Nan flew over the First World War Somme battlefields and then crossed the Oise River north of Paris. While no enemy aircraft were visible, their presence was unmistakeable, marked by more fiery deaths among the members of the bomber pack. There was no flak and no searchlights and the crew could only conclude that night fighters were preying on the bombers. Jack Currie explains:

> At listening posts in Britain the voice of the German night fighter controller came through clearly [in German]: 'Bombers are approaching the Amiens zone.' And a little later, 'bombers are entering the Beauvias zone'. The responses too were monitored: pilots of *I Gruppe NJG 4* at Florennes, and

of *II Gruppe* at Coulommiers, were orbiting their beacons and waiting instructions.[30]

The bombers were now approaching Reims and Colin throttled back as they reached the turning point to the south of the city. Slowly he guided the giant aircraft around to the south-east bombing path, dropping her to the bombing height of 5000 feet only to be told to re-orient and circle to the left, as the Pathfinder Mosquito bombers appeared to be late. They circled twice, their manoeuvre covered by operational orders which told them:

> H hour will be 0001hrs
>
> 5 Group A/C [aircraft] are to attack the SE half of the target in two waves between H+5 and H+11 minutes [467 Squadron was part of 5 Group]
>
> 1 Group A/C will be timed to arrive at the target at H+20 [some eventually attacked as part of 5 Group]
>
> From H+11 to H+20 no attack is to take place
>
> From H+20 to H+25 the NW half of the main target will be marked with red spot fires
>
> From H+26 No.1 Group main force aircraft are to aim their bombs at the red spot fires under the direction of No.5

Group M.C. [mission controller] on diversionary frequency

In the initial planning Nan was scheduled to be among the first few aircraft of the first wave, arriving over the target at H hour + four minutes. Nan's time over target was to be 12.05am. The Bomb Master, Wing Commander Leonard Cheshire, flying a Mosquito, was unhappy with the accuracy of the initial target marking and ordered the Pathfinder Mosquitos to circle again and re-mark the target, using the first group of target indication flares as reference points for the second marking.

However this disrupted the bombers' schedule and, between 5000 and 10,000 feet above the Aube countryside, chaos quickly ensued. What had begun as a routine bombing raid by 340 heavy bombers, a large number by French target standards, albeit far smaller than the Berlin raids of over 1000 bombers, was quickly unravelling and the bomber formation was about to be shot to pieces by the *Luftwaffe*, with German night fighters beginning to scythe into the pack. While initially the late arrival of the Pathfinders was blamed for the chaos, later evidence revealed that the bombers had in fact arrived early and the target re-marking, far from assisting the bombers, became a significant delaying factor. Radio communications between the aircraft were also problematic, with some radios off frequency while others proved incompatible, disrupting communication between the two bomber groups. Crews later reported their astonishment at finding that the airwaves were being jammed by a broadcast of Bing Crosby singing 'White Christmas'. The official explanation was that US forces were using radios with stronger signals which overwhelmed the aircraft frequency, although surviving crews believed that the Germans were also jamming the airways—a strange choice of jamming mode if this were the case. It was also apparent that some of the crews lacked radio discipline, filling the airwaves with questions and comments and receiving, in turn, short, sharp responses from Bombing Master Cheshire, directing them to 'cut the chat'.

The 'wooden wonder': three de Havilland Mosquito bombers of 21 Squadron, RAF, the same aircraft used by the Pathfinders on the Mailly raid (de Havilland Aviation Museum Trust collection).

Determining their true time over target proved extremely difficult for the crews in such a situation, with the men confronted by a maze of conflicting figures. Jack Currie, reviewing the mission later, notes that the first wave had just commenced its attack at 12.10am, which was the time the bombing should have been completed. Later reports reveal that the delay in reaching time over target varied from aircraft to aircraft and wave to wave. The length of the delay appears to have varied according to the bomber's position in the queue, with those towards the rear experiencing a more significant delay than those leading the formation.

Fortunately the bomb camera clocks were not affected by the delays and recorded the attack as it occurred. Naughty Nan was the third 467 Squadron bomber off the runway and Bob Hunter wrote later that it was the fourth 467 Squadron aircraft over the target. The bomb camera image records that the first 467 Squadron bomber over the target was flown by Pilot Officer Felsted whose time over target was just after 12.06am. The next two aircraft were recorded at 12.09am, with the fourth image captured by a 467 Squadron bomber taken at 12.10am. Squadron Leader Smith believed that he had been the first 467 Squadron bomber over the target at 12.06am rather than Felsted, but his bomb camera time is not recorded on the available lists. Allowing for Smith to be over the target at 12.06am, Naughty Nan must have arrived at around 12.09am, along with two other 467 Squadron aircraft, as expected of a bomber in the first and lowest wave.

A total of 42 Lancasters, one Mosquito and a Halifax bomber were lost in the raid. A plot of the crash points identified by Jack Currie indicates that at least eight bombers were shot down just east of Mailly during the period of circling while awaiting orders to proceed to bomb. Another seven bombers were shot down while circling further north in the vicinity of Châlons-sur-Marne.

The bomb camera time stamps confirm that the first aircraft were 90 seconds late over the target and the last of that group was nine minutes late. There were several stragglers before the second wave commenced bombing as scheduled at 12.26am.

By the time Nan lined up for her final approach, the scheduled time over target had been lost in the melee, and the aircraft was around four minutes late. Likewise, the tight aircraft formation had disintegrated while the bombers completed their circuits. However the bomb camera time stamps are consistent with the times recorded in the operations log following the post-operation interviews. Stan Jolly was in command of Naughty Nan, relaying directions back to Colin as the bomber was aligned onto its bombing path.

As Naughty Nan neared the target the bomb doors opened and the aircraft was rocked by the shock waves of the 4000lb bombs already exploding below. 'Bombs gone!' came the cry and the cameras immediately whirred and clicked into action. Colin simply had to hold Nan straight and level for the next 10 seconds. The cameras completed their task, the bomb bay doors closed, and the crew began to turn the aircraft to the right as they headed for home. A comparison between Nan's flight path and the navigation points provided suggests that Colin turned for home early. He was not the only one.

At this point the blazing fingers of searchlights appeared and Naughty Nan was soon coned in a shaft of light. As Colin began weaving to avoid the searchlights Stan noticed the impact line of tracer bullets on the right side of the aircraft as Nan was turning. Just as Colin was swinging Nan to the left in his weaving manoeuvre, desperate to avoid the searchlights, the aircraft was hit on the left-hand side, suggesting that a German fighter had attacked from behind. It is probable that, as Nan turned through the fall of shot from the fighter, the rear gunner, Hilton Forden, and Nan's mid-section were hit. Colin would not have been corkscrewing up to this point as he was avoiding the searchlights rather than attempting to shake off a fighter.

Night fighters usually loaded their guns with every second round a tracer. This assisted the attacking pilot to see the fall of shot and adjust onto the target accordingly. The attacking fighter, most probably a Focke-Wulf 190, was equipped with two 13mm MG131 machine-guns and four 20mm cannons with 250 rounds per gun (rpg) for the outer cannons and 140 rpg for the inner cannons. The MG131 machine-guns were capable of firing 15 rounds per second, so two machine-guns could fire 15 tracers per second between them. With 475 rpg these fighters carried sufficient ammunition for up to 30 seconds of continuous firing. The tracers also acted as an incendiary to ignite fuel and oil.

An extraordinary image from a bomb camera during the Mailly raid. The lack of a large fire suggests this photo was taken by one of the first aircraft over the target. Based on the perspective, the bomber visible is probably the last one at the minimum altitude of 5000 feet. Bomb camera records list no surviving bomber at this altitude, indicating this bomber was JA901 (RAF 1944 image).

The second burst hit Nan on the left wing and, as Bob Hunter wrote later, she 'shook like a tree in a windstorm' as the fuel tanks on her left wing erupted in flames.[31] 'Flames!' yelled a crew member, most likely the mid-upper gunner, Jack Skellorn, as he had the best field of view. The area forward of his section of the aircraft was soon ablaze. Colin immediately told Taffy to feather the engines. This was the same action he had adopted a fortnight earlier when the crew had lost an engine soon after take-off.

Stan recalled later that he could not see the fire and that the aircraft was still flying 'normally' when Colin Dickson called to Taffy to 'feather the props' and the crew to 'abandon the kite'.[32] But all now knew that Nan was in trouble.

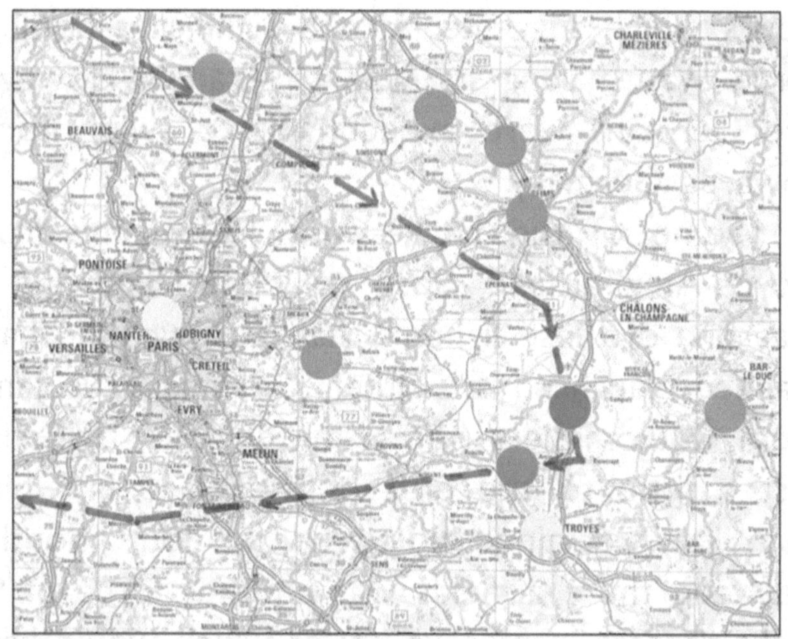


Map of Nan's final flight. Broken line: the clockwise flight path to the target and return home. Right dot on flight path indicates target. Lower dot indicates point where Naughty Nan was lost. Dot left of centre is Paris, where Stan Jolly hid for 4 months. Other dots indicate German fighter bases.

The map provides a clear indication of the trouble that the German night fighters, primarily Junkers JU88, Messerschmitt Bf-110s and Focke-Wulf 190s, were set to cause. All these aircraft were radio direction and radar-equipped. The noise footprint of the first wave of 170 heavy bombers passing Montdidier (the top left green dot) would have been sufficient for the other five airfields to scramble their fighters. This decision would have been supported by German monitoring of radio traffic over the previous hours which suggested that a significant bomber force was making its way to France. However the Germans were expecting it to swing north towards Germany.

Some of the Focke-Wulf 190s came from Royce-Amy airfield close to Montdidier and it was one of these fighters that is thought to have claimed Naughty Nan. Other 190s and 110s came from Coulommiers (the green dot east of Paris), just a little to the east of the place in which Stan Jolly remained holed up for four months. Between these airfields was another force of 92 night fighters in reserve, 60 of which would have been serviceable at any one time.

That Wednesday night—3 May 1944—a total of 352 bombers of all types took off on what was the biggest mission into France to date. By daybreak on 4 May, 12.5% of the mission—some 44 bombers—had been lost. The highest bomber loss was 13.5% on 'Black Thursday', 16/17 December 1943, during a disastrous mission to Berlin. The Mailly-le-Camp mission resulted in the deaths of 257 aircrew, while 24 became prisoners of war and just 34 evaded the Germans and eventually made their way back to England. The horrific losses of that night rewrote the guidelines for bombing missions into France.

# CHAPTER 10

# THE AFTERMATH

With Naughty Nan well ablaze, her crew now staged a desperate fight for survival. Given Bomber Command's horrific casualty rate, all aircrew were well drilled in escaping from a stricken aircraft. The same could not be said for parachute training. Indeed, a boy falling out of a tree had as much experience of falling from a height as these young airmen had gained in the training designed to teach them to execute a parachute jump. Stan Jolly wrote later that his training consisted of strapping on a parachute harness and perching on a box standing around one foot (30 centimetres) high, from which he was instructed to fall off and roll as he hit the ground. It was as simple as that, he was reassured. Stan was to discover for himself just how far his training was removed from the stark reality of jumping from a stricken bomber.

With Nan hit and her crew now instructed to bale out, Stan attempted to open the forward escape hatch beneath the front gunner/bomb aimer's feet. As he did so, he became aware of the boots of fellow crewman Taffy coming down the steps into the forward compartment. With an airspeed of over 200mph at this point the wind pressure on the nose of the bomber was enormous. Stan managed to force the door open and attempted to rotate it and push it out into the air stream as he had been trained. However the immense wind pressure forced the door back into its aperture, wedging it tight in a vertical position. The escape hatch is 70 centimetres by 60 centimetres clear but, with the door jammed vertically reducing the size of the hole, Stan could not fit through. With his life flashing before him and thoughts of the distress of his mother and fiancée should he be lost, Stan found the energy to kick the wedged hatch cover across sufficiently to slip through the hole and into the beckoning night sky. By this time Nan had dropped to around 5000 feet, a low but safe altitude for a parachute novice.

The forward escape hatch in a Lancaster bomber. Stan had to pull the large ring on the hatch marked 'parachute exit' and force the hatch into the airstream. In a subsequent redesign of the escape hatch, the ring pull was replaced by a lever which was easier to use (author image).

The instructions for exiting through the front hatch were relatively straightforward: squat on the floor, tuck the head down and tumble out. It was important that the exiting aircrew avoid cracking their heads on the trailing edge of the escape hatch. The restricted gap meant than Stan had to sit on the edge of the hole with his feet dangling out, thread his body through the now-constricted hole without damaging his parachute and finally let go—remembering where the parachute 'D handle' was. Stan could now see the flames threatening to engulf the aircraft and was concerned that he would be severely burnt, although he ultimately escaped without injury.[33]

Once Stan was out of the aircraft he felt the jolt as his parachute opened and watched with horror as Nan disappeared into the dark, the aircraft soon engulfed by a ball of fire. In the gloom that surrounded the blazing bomber he watched as another parachute opened in the distance and at a far lower altitude. His attention returned to the fireball that had been Naughty Nan and he watched her turn sharply left, losing altitude quickly, but flattening as she fell, as if to come in for a soft landing. Then a smaller fireball flew off to the left. Stan formed the impression that the left wing had broken off as the aircraft ploughed nose first into the ground some 1400 metres east and on the Mailly side of the tiny village of Droupt-Sainte-Marie.

Bob Hunter's escape from the wireless operator position was no less traumatic. Bob had clipped on his parachute and prepared to move forward to the escape hatch. He looked up at Oscar who was standing in front of him. Oscar had donned his parachute but stood motionless, as if unable to move, clearly unsure of which direction to take. Bob knew he had to move quickly. He noted that the forward escape route looked blocked—there were four crewmen between his station and the escape hatch with Taffy halfway down the ladder into the front compartment. He knew there was no time to wait in queue while the others jumped.

He turned, deciding to use the rear escape hatch, unaware of what lay on the other side of the draught wall between the main spar hump and the rear crew positions. Bob was a very fit man with amateur boxing experience and he quickly hurdled the centre spar and flung open the door in the draught partition only to meet a wall of flame which engulfed the centre of the aircraft. He turned again to reconsider an escape from the front but the crewmen remained blocking his path. Oscar had not moved, still apparently unsure of which way to turn while Taffy stood, still halfway down the ladder. Bob knew immediately that he had no choice.

Forcing his way through the flames, severely burning both hands on hot metal as he tried to brace himself against the motion of the pitching and rolling bomber, Bob pushed back through the aircraft. He glanced up and noticed Jack Skellorn, the mid-upper gunner, who was out of his turret and standing, holding onto the turret with both hands. His head was lowered between his arms and, in what appeared a hopelessly futile gesture, he kicked at the flames licking his boots. He was not wearing his parachute.

Bob later recalled glimpsing the rear turret through the smoke and fire, noting that it was pointing towards the rear of the aircraft, the rear gunner's parachute still hanging on its hook. There was no visible movement in the turret. He could only conclude that Hilton Forden had been killed in the attack by the night fighter.

By now Bob had managed to make his way through the burning aircraft and grabbed the rear door handle with his badly burnt left hand, giving it a twist. It remained solidly closed. Bob jerked at the handle a few times, his desperation mounting. He gave the door an almighty wrench and, while the door still refused to budge, the force of his wrench was sufficient to punch him through both the floor and outer skin of the aircraft. The movement sent his lower body right through the aircraft and it was only his parachute catching on the airframe that prevented him being pitched into the night sky.

There is approximately a handspan of space between the floor of the aircraft and its outer skin at the rear door. The rear door itself was made of wood, designed to burn quickly to allow an easier exit. Bob had attempted to open the door with his left hand when facing the rear of the aircraft, the direction in which he was running. As he dangled in the hole, the wind stream caught Bob's lower body and turned him around. He was now facing forward with his knees bent and his heels swinging up towards the fuselage. His shredded trousers were torn off his body by the wind and he was naked from the Mae West down.

By now Bob was utterly exhausted and had all but lost hope of getting out of the aircraft alive. But thoughts of his mother spurred him to make one last effort to free himself. Fuelled by desperation, he rocked back and kicked upwards, while pushing down on the hot metal floor around him and, with a giant thrust, strove to propel himself back inside the burning aircraft. This time he succeeded. The rear door now opened easily and Bob was free of Nan just before she erupted in flames on impact with a small stand of trees. The hole Bob created when he punctured the floor may have been sufficient to alter the balance of air pressure in the aircraft, freeing the door and allowing it to be opened.

Bob grabbed at the D handle a dozen times with his badly burnt hand before he succeeded in pulling it hard enough to open the parachute.

He was later to lose the little finger on each hand. The doctor in Troyes took one look at the charred condition of his hands and, with toxic blood now pumping through his body, declared that the only option was to amputate both hands.[34]

The crash of Lancaster bomber N-Nan into a grove of trees close to the village of Droupt-Sainte-Marie was reported to the German authorities at 12.25am. It had taken less than 20 minutes for the aircraft to drop her deadly payload, sustain a hit and die in a spectacular blaze, taking most of her crew with her.

Colin Dickson may never have seen the fighter that shot Naughty Nan out of the sky, but he could certainly see the searchlight beams in front of him. Stan Jolly noted that the beams of searchlights were both in front of and behind them. The crew were well practised in weaving in and out of searchlights, the primary lesson from the bull's eye training run, in which pilots slide and weave their aircraft away from the darting, stabbing lights. The corkscrew manoeuvre is designed to turn the aircraft quickly and sharply inside the cone of a searchlight or the trajectory of a fighter's bullets. While a fighter is a great deal more agile than a lumbering bomber, its speed is often much higher and thus its turning circle is greater. Any but the most experienced fighter pilots would often break off an engagement with a bomber as, once spotted, the bomber's highly rotatable gun turrets allow the gunners to maintain their aim on an attacking fighter. On the bull's eye run a week earlier, Colin Dickson had reported that the bomber in front of him had been engaged by two JU88s and successfully fought them off.

In a recording made for the Australian War Memorial, Flight Lieutenant Frank Dixon, a pilot with 467 Squadron, described the techniques for evading pursuing fighters:

> Well you can't do a lot about evading. You take evasive action if you're quick when the first one hits you, you can get out of it fairly quickly because he's got to wait until you move before he knows which way you're going and so on, but you've got a stream of aircraft coming in great concentration so you can't go running around in circles and that sort of thing, because you run into your mates. So what you do is slide off to the right or left or you go up a bit or down a bit, but you keep your general direction and your general activity.
>
> We had a process which was called 'weaving'. We went about fifteen degrees to the left and you climbed a bit and you

> rolled over to the right and you went about fifteen degrees to the right and you descended as you went there, but you kept doing that in some balance, not in a regular equal balance because then the smart bloke would predict your move. But you did thirty seconds to the left this time and forty-five seconds to the right and then forty-five seconds to the left and then thirty seconds to the right and roughly maintained a balance, but not in any regular pattern.[35]

Colin clearly had Naughty Nan in a weaving manoeuvre. Stan noted that he first saw tracers on the right-hand side but could not see the fighter. With the second burst of fire from the fighter however, he heard the drum of bullets hitting metal just above his head. By the time Colin gave the order to abandon the aircraft the left side of the bomber was shot up and ablaze. However Bob Hunter was unaware of the fire inside the fuselage until he opened the draught door. From the vantage points of their parachutes, both Stan and Bob noted that the left-hand wing and fuel tanks were blazing fiercely before Naughty Nan erupted into a fireball and appeared to break up as she hit the ground.

Given that Stan saw tracers but not the fighter, it is likely that it attacked from behind and possibly above Nan. In fact, it is highly probable that the German fighter attacked from the right rear while Nan was dodging searchlights and hit the rear gunner with the first volley. The fact that the fighter attacked from the rear, firing first to the right and then to the left side of the bomber confirms that Nan was turning to the left as Colin weaved to dodge the searchlights. As the aircraft turned further to the left, the fall of shot from the fighter hit first the wings and then the front of the aircraft, the volleys of bullets also hitting the mid-upper turret area. The broken hydraulic lines in this area indicate a combination of shrapnel and incendiary tracers bouncing around inside the aircraft, further damaging the hydraulic turret drive lines and igniting the hydraulic oil and other flammables. As Nan swung further to the left and the left side became exposed, the left wing and fuel tanks were hit and this is probably the volley that Stan heard above his head. At this halfway point in the mission, Nan is likely to have had over 800 gallons of fuel remaining in her tanks—enough for a grand fire. Certainly the middle of the plane was well ablaze by the time Bob moved towards the rear door to jump.

Captured German documents record Nan as being shot down over 'Merz on Seine', 14 kilometres south of 'Romilly'. Allowing for errors in the German rendering of French names, the report most likely refers to Méry-sur-Seine, 14 kilometres east of Romilly-sur-Seine. Méry-sur-Seine is located some five kilometres west of where Nan crashed.

*Luftwaffe* High Command fighter claims for 3/4 May do not identify any point of engagement as 'Merz on Seine', but do record one kill at between 50 and 60 kilometres south-east of the tiny village of Champlion. Champlion sits close to a small wooded ridgeline northeast of Coulommiers, a major *Luftwaffe* fighter airfield east-south-east of Paris. The reference to Champlion suggests that there was probably a *Luftwaffe* radar installation on the ridgeline. The point 50 to 60 kilometres south-east of Champlion is Romilly-sur-Seine.

Bob Hunter pinpoints the attack on Nan as three to four minutes after the bomber's time on target, suggesting that the time of the attack was around 12.13 to 12.14am.[36] Stan also noted that the bomber was attacked soon after turning for home, just as Colin began weaving through the searchlights.[37] RAF records of interviews with the two evaders (Bob Hunter and Stan Jolly) placed the time Nan was attacked as between midnight and 1.00am. Several other reports on file record the time of the attack as 12.30am. According to the residents of

Droupt-Sainte-Marie, the Germans received notification of the crash of JA901 at 12.25am.

As quickly becomes evident, establishing the precise time of the attack is no easy matter. An attack and crash at around 12.30am, for example, occurs too late after the time on target relative to Nan's position. An attack time of 15 minutes after the time on target at an assumed bomber speed of 200mph (320kph) would have placed Nan 80 kilometres away from the target, much closer to the south of Paris. From Mailly-le-Camp to the crash site is around 30 kilometres. Considering the available ground evidence, the time of 12.15am for the fighter attack is the most feasible.

The flight path over the target took the bombers from the northwest to the south-east. Colin began turning for home soon after the bomb doors closed, identifiably earlier than the turning point stipulated in the operational orders, possibly to avoid the searchlights he could see ahead. Nan was certainly seen overhead close to the little village of Premierfait and crashed 1.4 kilometres north-east of Droupt-Sainte-Marie. Turning soon after closing the bomb doors suggests a steady, curved flight path some 12 kilometres south of Mailly and then over Premierfait and Droupt-Sainte-Marie. The primary rule was not to turn back into the path of the following bombers. Both evaders mention that Colin held Nan level after the bombs were dropped and both believed they jumped at 5000 feet. Nan's altitude at the time of the attack was around 5500 feet. Neither evader mentions Nan climbing or corkscrewing. When interviewed by the RAF, the Mayor of Premierfait made no mention of seeing parachutes as the burning aircraft flew overhead, suggesting that the evaders had jumped prior to the flight of the blazing bomber over the village.

Interestingly, the *Luftwaffe* kept such detailed and accurate records that it is possible to identify the pilot who was probably responsible for shooting Nan down. *Oberfeldwebel* (Flight Sergeant) Tirchow of *3./SKG10,* flying out of Roye-Amy airfield close to Montdidier, claimed a Lancaster 'kill' 12 kilometres south of Mailly-le-Camp at 12.15am and at 3200 metres (10,500 feet). Tirchow flew a Focke-Wulf 190A and this was his first combat kill as a *Luftwaffe* pilot.

Bombing generally occurred from between 5000 and 8000 feet. Allowing for a target height of 500 feet above sea level, this altitude becomes 5500 feet (1680 metres) to 8500 feet (2600 metres). The *Luftwaffe* records show attacking altitudes between 1000 metres (3200 feet) and 4000 metres (13,000 feet), with half of the bombers attacking at or over 3000 metres (9800 feet). Records of attack altitudes appear to be inconsistent with the probable height of engagement and may indicate the height at which the fighter was patrolling.

Both evaders report that Nan climbed once the bombs were released and then dropped to between 6000 and 5000 feet before they jumped. Between these two events Colin had been weaving to avoid the searchlights so it is highly probable that Nan was above 2000 metres (6600 feet) when first seen by the *Luftwaffe* fighter patrolling at 3000 metres (9800 feet).

Tirchow's claim of a Lancaster 'kill' 12 kilometres south of Maillyle-Camp at 12.15am is consistent with the available data on Nan. All reports also indicate that Colin Dickson was able to maintain some control of Nan, now flying on the two starboards engines only, while the crew fought to escape, thus allowing for the distance between the point of the attack and the final crash site.

Dickson turned for home some 12 kilometres south-east of the target, much earlier than the point specified in the operations orders as 34 kilometres south of the target. During most missions it was normal for the aircraft to turn for home as soon as the bombs were released and the doors closed. Certainly at least one other aircraft also turned early, as Stan heard another bomber overhead while he was descending in his parachute. Being in the first group over the target and turning early would have separated Nan from the cluster of aircraft heading south towards Troyes before turning and this may have exposed Nan and made her more vulnerable to fighter attack. Of the six 467 Squadron bombers over the target in the first cluster, Nan was the only aircraft not to return safely to Waddington.

The army barracks and their attached messes, workshops and offices that had been the target of the raid were almost completely demolished and German archives recorded total casualties in the camp as 218 killed or missing and 156 wounded, a high proportion of these German Army NCOs. Some 102 vehicles, including 37 tanks, were also destroyed. Of the buildings in the barracks area, almost 80% were deemed beyond repair, the remainder likely to take some time and substantial effort to rebuild.

The aftermath of the raid, a photograph taken on 6 May 1944. The severely damaged army barracks are visible in the top right corner.

Oblique angle photograph taken a few days after the raid, possibly from a Spitfire or Mosquito (images courtesy of the Mailly Association).

Casualties from the raid were roughly equivalent between the two belligerents, with the total number of Germans killed and wounded approximating the 258 bomber crew killed and the 50 who evaded or were taken prisoner. However the local French population was also hit hard and suffered a number of casualties although, at the time, this was not revealed to the public. The original official statement from the RAF declared that 'No French civilians were killed in the bombing, although there were a small number of casualties when one of the Lancasters shot down crashed on their house.' The bombing was deliberately conducted from a very low height to maximise accuracy and minimise the possibility of villagers being killed.

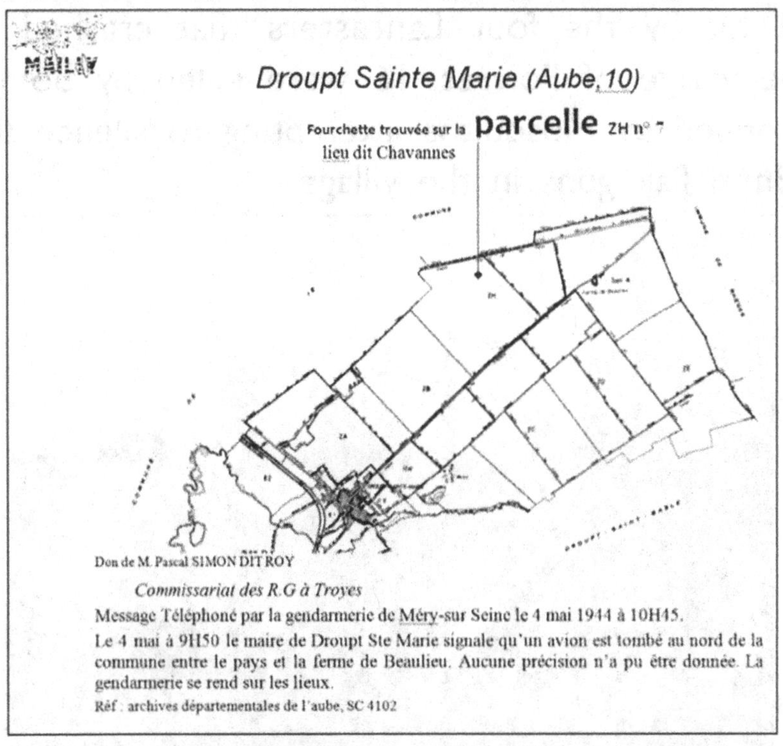


A sketch map alongside the original crash report as recorded by the local French authority (archives départementales de l'aube, SC 4102 image).

However, French sources provide an altogether different picture of the local civilian casualties, listing French losses as 109 killed and 23 injured. The dead included 41 French colonial soldiers who were prisoners of war and 10 of their dependants, 30 forced labourers who worked in the camp, and four civilians in the village of Mailly-le-Camp itself. Outside the village, another two were killed and 23 injured close to

Châlons-en-Champagne, five were killed at Trouans, and one at Beauchery-Saint-Martin, all 31 hit by the four Lancasters that crashed. In the village of Poivres, 16 were killed by bombs dropped by Mosquitos attempting to silence the 88mm flak guns in the village.

Field of impact near Droupt-Sainte-Marie, 1400 metres from the church (author image).

Yet the local French people bore no ill will towards the RAF aircrew who wreaked such havoc on the night of 3 May 1944. Instead, they regarded the men as courageous for risking their lives in the fight to liberate France from the German invaders. The French also recognised that the aircrews had done their utmost to guide their stricken aircraft away from population centres to protect the lives of the local people. This had often cost them their own lives as they had remained inside the burning bombers until it was too late to bale out. As Isabelle Farcy, the youngest witness to the raid, at two and a half years of age, remarked later:

> The bombing of the 3-4 May 1944 is one of my first childhood remembrances ... Maybe I am the youngest witness, and I remember that dreadful night by flashes. My uncle helped to rescue Jack Worsfold who survived the crash of his shot down plane as rear gunner badly injured ... I [later] discovered that the airmen had a priority not to kill any villager, and they took risks for that ... [38]

To the local French these men were heroes and they became a revered part of the history of the villages, their graves lovingly tended to this day.

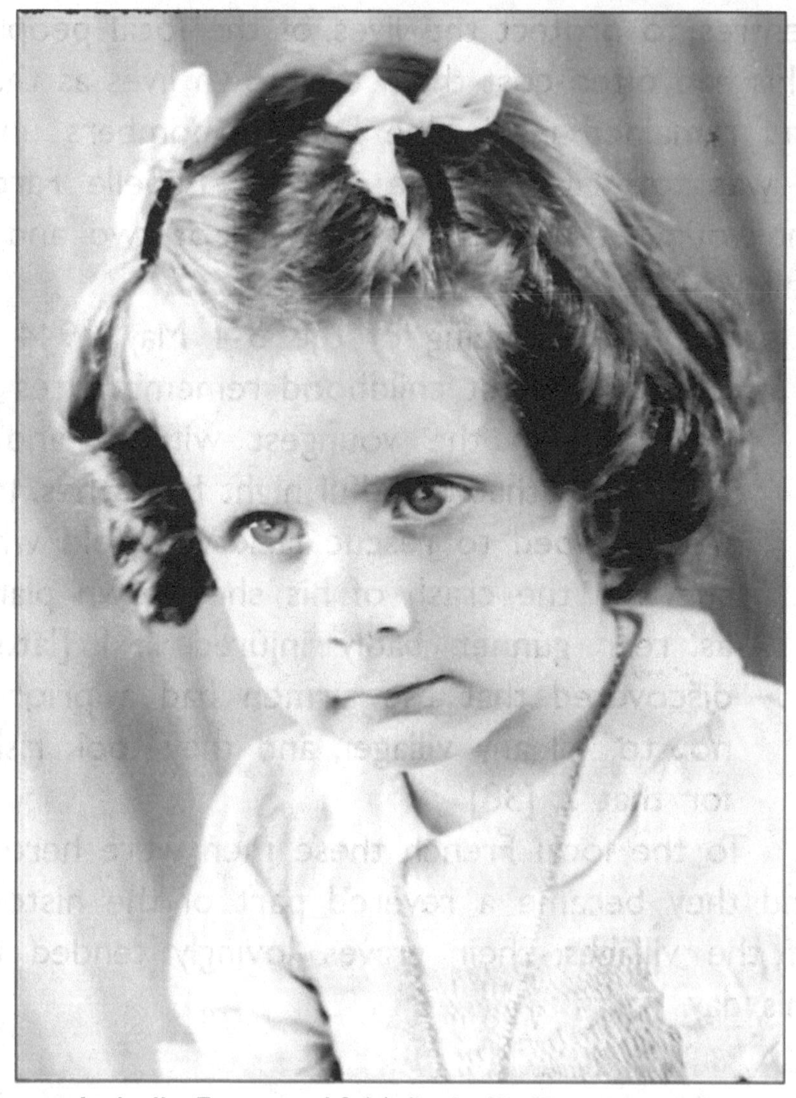

Isabelle Farcy in 1944 (Isabelle Farcy image).

# CHAPTER 11

# THE FATE OF THE CREW

The Lancaster had four designated escape hatches and an access door to the rear on the right-hand side. Stan escaped through the hatch located in the nose of the aircraft while Bob jumped through the rear access door. There were two hatches in the roof along the fuselage, one each side of the draught door, and a third in the centre of the pilot's canopy. This last hatch was located in the roof behind the pilot, and was intended for use by the pilot, engineer and navigator. During Naughty Nan's last moments there was clearly no attempt to use any of these three roof hatches and there were very good reasons for this. Access to these escape points in an aircraft pitching and rolling in an emergency situation would have been extremely difficult. Even had the crewmen successfully escaped through these hatches, they may then have been blown into the spinning propellers or the tail wing and fins. These roof hatches were designed primarily to allow aircrew to extricate themselves from stationary aircraft.

Stan slipped through the front escape hatch and, as his canopy billowed, he watched horrified as his beloved Naughty Nan turned into a ball of fire. He was also searching for the parachutes that signalled the escape of his fellow crew members and it would have been with some relief that he greeted the sight of a second parachute as it opened far below him. At the time, Stan thought this was Taffy Weaver. Both evaders report seeing Nan turn sharply left and drop altitude as if coming in to land. Then both watched a second ball of fire fall away as she hit the ground. Stan believed this may have been the left wing breaking off. What they would not have seen in the glare of the flames, obscured by their distance from the crash, was the tail section breaking off at the moment of impact.

In a letter to Colin Dickson's father dated 12 March 1945, the RAAF Directorate of Personnel Services' Casualty Section stated that 'The possibility that the aircraft exploded cannot be overlooked and I regret to advise you that such an explosion, if it took place, may have rendered impossible an identification of the aircraft or its occupants.' This assertion is based on an RAF report from an interview with the evaders following their arrival in London. Certainly the shock of such an explosion would have knocked any surviving crew members unconscious, particularly those not strapped into the aircraft, and they would not have experienced the final moments of impact.

Hilton Forden, the rear gunner, was almost certainly dead by the time Bob Hunter jumped. As Bob noted, the rear turret was pointing straight back and Hilton's parachute was still hanging on its hook beside the turret. This suggests that the night fighter had been directly behind Naughty Nan as she turned and that Hilton had been hit by enemy fire, probably the first burst, and may have been killed instantly. When the bodies were exhumed five years later, Hilton Forden's identity was confirmed by his dog tags, indicating that he was not burnt.

Horace 'Jack' Skellorn was the mid-upper gunner and was last seen by Bob Hunter as he scrambled to escape the burning bomber. Bob described Jack as standing on the floor of the aircraft, holding onto the upper turret with both hands, his head lowered between his arms. He had not clipped on his parachute. This appears to suggest that Jack was critically wounded—perhaps even losing consciousness as he stood gripping the turret. He had certainly responded to Colin Dickson's call to 'abandon the kite', although he appears to have been too badly wounded to do more than clamber out of his turret. Climbing into and out of the turret was no easy matter. While it is impossible to determine whether Jack was hit by enemy fire or the shrapnel that ricocheted through his crew space, he had certainly been hit by one or the other, possibly both. The rear door that Bob was eventually able to open and through which he ultimately escaped is a mere two paces from the mid-upper gun turret. However there must have been a considerable draught through the aircraft and a significant aerodynamic disturbance once Bob opened the rear door. Jack was still inside the bomber when the Germans reached the crash site, so he had clearly been unable to use this easy exit point. It is probably safe to conclude that he lost consciousness quickly.

When the bodies were exhumed five years later, the British Missing Research and Enquiries Unit (MREU) was able to confirm Jack's identity from remnants of his RAF uniform. Again this points to the fact that his body had not been charred in the blaze. The fact that neither the rear gunner nor the mid-upper gunner were burnt suggests that the tail section of the bomber broke off somewhere near the mid-upper gun turret and fell clear of the fire, allowing the Germans to retrieve these two bodies as the remainder of the bomber burned. Both gunners were in the tail section which fell clear of the main fireball when it hit the ground.

Colin Dickson was the only crew member not observed by either evader. Colin was firmly strapped into his seat and his final moments can only be conjectured from Nan's flight behaviour and the observation of Monsieur M.C. Drouard, Mayor of Premierfait, who saw the burning bomber pass overhead. The pilot's task in such a situation is to maintain level flight to the best of his ability to enable all the other crew members to escape. As they descended, both Stan and Bob noted that Nan appeared to be holding a steady flight path—so steady, in fact, that both noted its resemblance to a quick descent before a controlled landing. The sudden lurch to the left at the end could have been Colin Dickson's desperate attempt to avoid the village of Droupt-Sainte-Marie, which lay directly in the flight path just 1400 metres and 13 seconds ahead. The evidence suggests that Colin did not leave his seat and, while it is possible that he had been wounded by the second volley of shots that Stan heard spattering overhead, his last moments in Naughty Nan were nothing short of heroic and certainly worthy of recognition. All reports identify Colin as a talented young pilot with extraordinary flying skills and he clearly deserved these accolades.

According to Stan Jolly, flight engineer Philip 'Taffy' Weaver was coming down the steps into the forward compartment as Stan himself struggled to create sufficient room in the forward escape hatch to exit the burning bomber. Stan's description of how he ultimately escaped, by threading himself down through the gap between the jammed escape door and the wall of the aircraft, suggests that the gap was very small, far smaller than the hatch size of 60 centimetres by 70 centimetres. Taffy was 10 years older than the rest of the crew and his torso was more mature and better developed. Stan's account of the size of the hatch suggests that Taffy was simply too large to fit through the now much-reduced escape hole while wearing his parachute. In fact it is probable that Taffy became wedged while trying to force his way through the hole.

Access to the forward compartment is through the space under the pedals of the second pilot's position on the right. Taffy was standing on the top step below the pedals. The escape hole is clearly visible (author image).

Navigator Oscar Furniss was certainly wearing his parachute the last time Bob Hunter saw him. Twice Bob glanced at Oscar, each time assessing that, while he was standing and wearing his parachute, he appeared unsure of which way to move, perhaps blindsided by the fact that there was no movement around the escape hatch forward of his position. Bob's flinging the draught door open to reveal the raging fire must have compounded Oscar's bewilderment; he now knew that he had nowhere to go with the front exit blocked by Taffy and the rear of the aircraft ablaze. Had the fuel exploded—which is possible—the explosion would have flung Oscar against the side of the aircraft, possibly knocking him unconscious. It is impossible, however, to make an informed assessment of Oscar's final moments.

Wireless operator Bob Hunter certainly had some terrifying moments before he was able to open the rear escape door and tumble out. Bob had assessed that his best option for escape was through the rear door rather than the blocked front hatch. He hurdled the centre spar, threw the draught door open and was immediately confronted by the fire. He was then forced to stop and check all the possible means of escape, turning to look forward and noticing Oscar still standing motionless while Taffy remained blocking the forward route. Bob made his decision and ran directly through the flames. He fell through the floor and, having mentally abandoned hope, managed to recoup his energy with thoughts of home. That adrenalin surge allowed him to propel himself from the hole in the floor back into the aircraft, open the rear door and jump, sometime after Stan escaped from the front hatch. Bob fell a long way before he managed to open his parachute, his burnt hands preventing him pulling the D handle for several crucial seconds. He was concerned that he was too low for his parachute to open effectively, but open it did and he was the first to reach the ground.

Baling out of a Lancaster via the side door at 400kph is fraught with danger as Flying Officer Frank 'Tim' Haddlesey, DFC, RCAF, was to discover. Tim was Jack Colpus' mid-upper gunner and had often flown in Naughty Nan. On 18 July 1944 he flew with another crew in PO-F for a mission to Revigny on the French border with Switzerland. The aircraft was shot down over France and Tim baled out through the side door only to be struck by the tail fin as he fell, severely injuring his leg. Once he landed he was picked up by the French Resistance which, unsurprisingly, lacked the medical resources to treat such a major wound. Tim was eventually taken to a German field hospital where doctors discovered that his leg had become gangrenous. At the time this discovery was made, he was also visited by a high-ranking German officer who Tim asserts was none other than *Reichsmarschall* Herman Göring. The German officer asked the doctors why they had yet to treat the stricken airman, only to be told that, since he was RAF, he was considered less urgent. The horrified German officer issued orders for the young airman to be taken to a proper hospital for treatment and Tim credits this with saving his life. Tim's leg was amputated and he was later fitted with a wooden leg. He finished his war in a prisoner-of-war camp.[39]

Front gunner/bomb aimer Stan Jolly would have experienced anxiety levels at least as elevated as those of the severely burnt Bob Hunter. Stan, however, was positioned immediately above his point of escape and, despite his enormous difficulty pulling himself through the restricted escape hole, he was the first to bale out of the aircraft. As Stan drifted to earth he longed for the England he thought he would never see again.

The loss of an aircraft and crew was always deeply felt by the remaining members of the squadron and also by those from other squadrons with whom they had trained. For Flight Lieutenant Noel Sanders of 463 Squadron this was a dark day indeed. Colin and Noel were lifelong friends, having met during their first days at school in Kempsey, New South Wales.

After each operation the crew were interviewed as part of the preparation of a post-operation report. The interviewers were intelligence officers, generally female NCOs, who then compiled the reports in the various logs. On 4 May 1944, the 467 Squadron log recorded a sobering entry:

> Bad news—this time it's F/Sgt [sic] Dickson who failed to return. His was a

new crew and were just settling down nicely and doing a good job. Visibility was good but the fighter activity was intense. Aircraft were going down everywhere and it was feared that losses will be high. It was however an excellent prang [i.e. the target was successfully destroyed].

The open front escape hatch, located under the front gunner/bomb aimer (author image).

Reports from the other crews also included in the squadron operations log describe the conditions in which the raid was conducted:

> ...Good concentration of red spot flares on buildings themselves ... Bombs fell across same buildings. According to crew it should be a successful raid. Controller said bombing was rather wild to start but later on he seemed very satisfied both with bombing and markers ... Aiming point seen to be hit

> by bomb aimer. Marking of target excellent and on very good time. Order to attack received clearly over R/T [radio]. Attack very well organised, carried out and bombed ... Defences around target negligible and PFF [Pathfinder Force marking] very accurate although controller not heard on W/T [wireless telegraphy]. Plenty of fighter activity around the target ... No heavy flak and only one light gun in target area, and no S/L [searchlights].

One report, from Pilot Officer McManus, was however, very telling:

> ...Consider most of the A/C [aircraft] lost in this attack were shot down while circling target area waiting to bomb. Target tactics definitely considered unnecessary. A/c should be timed to bomb within 5 minutes of zero thus eliminating the half hour orbit which caused unnecessary losses. Consider one third of an operation most unjust...

Added Pilot Officer Coulson:

> ...Still rather unsatisfactory being kept around target area. As a result Jerry seemed to collect a few fighters in area which reaped quite a harvest. If this is still a third of a trip I'm verging on L.M.F. [lack of moral fibre]

Flight Lieutenant Jack Colpus' final tribute to Nan was to build this model of the aircraft after his posting to 27 Officer Training Unit at Lichfield on the completion of his 30 missions in May 1944 (author image).

And from aircraft JA901, there was no report. The entry simply stated: 'P/O Dickson. Aircraft missing. No message received.

The bond between aircrew formed very quickly and generally lasted a lifetime. This is not surprising since each life was totally dependent on the competency of the other six aircrew. The aircrew's affection for 'their' aircraft was often just as strong regardless of how they rated its performance. The two aircrew who survived Nan's loss in France spoke of her with affection despite also describing her as an 'unreliable kite'. Likewise, Flight Lieutenant Jack Colpus, DFC, who flew Nan more often than any other pilot, cursed her unreliability with more than a small degree of affection. Jack first flew Nan on her second mission following her return from her extended stay in Africa, noting later in his log book that she was in poor condition given a lack of servicing at Biskra. One faulty engine had been replaced by a Spitfire engine (which had completely different performance characteristics), and some routine upgrades had not been completed. With Nan requiring careful attention after every second mission, Jack was soon pleading with the CO of 467 Squadron for another aircraft. This plea was answered on 18 April 1944 when Jack was assigned to a new Lancaster, PO-D (LL843), after Colin Dickson and crew arrived at the squadron. Jack wrote in his log book after his first flight in his new aircraft that she was 'a joy to fly compared to "N" Nan', before noting that a 1000lb bomb had not released cleanly. In another entry, Jack added that his new aircraft could climb to 20,000 feet with ease and the crew were now more confident of returning from a mission. Jack's affection for Nan clearly continued however, as he added a sad note to his log following news that Nan had been lost on 3 May 1944.[40]

# CHAPTER 12

# THE IMPACT ON THE FAMILIES

Because Nan was shot down deep inside German-occupied territory, there was a considerable delay before information was available to the families of the aircrew. On Thursday 4 May 1944 RAAF Headquarters was advised that aircraft JA901 was missing, having not returned from a raid over Mailly-le-Camp in France, and that the fate of its crew was unknown. The report added that the aircraft's loss was presumed to be the result of enemy action.

By Saturday 6 May, the RAAF office in South Yarra, Melbourne, had been advised that several Australian aircrew had been posted as missing. Immediately a telegram was sent to the local Post Office of the next of kin listed against each of Naughty Nan's aircrew. In Wentworth Falls the telegram appeared on the little machine in the Post Office, as luck would have it, arriving while the Post Office was closed for the weekend. The news that would shatter a family remained undisclosed as Oscar's parents and siblings enjoyed a soft autumn day, the crisp mountain air now laden with the smoke of burning leaves as the local gardeners built little bonfires, joyfully poked and prodded by their whooping offspring. As Monday dawned and the offices of the little town opened to greet the working week, it was the postmistress who first received the news. This was a small, tightly knit community and she was well aware just how devastating the news would be for Oscar and Bertha Furniss. She made a cup of strong, sweet tea and sat down to compose herself. This time she could not send the telegram boy—after all, the Furniss family lived just metres away on the other side of the laneway—she would deliver the dreadful news herself. That much she owed Oscar and Bertha.

By 9.35 the postmistress had finished her cup of tea, rehearsed a little speech brim full of condolences, closed the Post Office temporarily and launched herself into the shop across the lane—Barr & Furniss Real Estate. In the family rooms above the real estate office the postmistress knew she would find Bertha immersed in her morning chores. In the office she found Oscar and ushered him upstairs, grateful that, for once, he had seen fit not to argue. Something in her manner had robbed him of his fire.

'The Minister for Air joins with the Air Board in expressing sincere sympathy in your anxiety' read the carefully worded telegram. Oscar and Bertha stood transfixed. Bertha's shock soon gave way to heavy sobs that shook her entire body, but Oscar was jolted into life. The telegram had mentioned their 'anxiety'—after all, he reasoned, his son had been reported missing, not confirmed dead. He was always reading reports in the newspapers describing the adventures of airmen who had been shot down over enemy territory and miraculously evaded capture, ultimately finding their way back to England. Why should his boy be any different?

But Bertha remained unconvinced. She was consumed by a deep, boundless grief that even the local vicar could not shift. What her family failed to understand was that the death of her son had also destroyed her hopes of a new life away from the mundanity of the real estate office. Her vision of living out her days on a little farm with Oscar and his family had been shattered in a single night by an event she could not comprehend in a distant land she had only ever read about. She mourned her lost son and her lost dream in equal measure. As Oscar's sister Muriel, who was a member of the WAAAF in Kiama at the time recalls, her mother's grief was overwhelming and soon engulfed her father.

When the passing of days brought no further news, the door of Barr & Furniss Real Estate in Wentworth Falls was closed and the grieving started in earnest.

On 7 June a letter of condolence written by Squadron Leader D.P. Smith, temporary CO of 467 Squadron, reached the family. The letter was dated 5 May, and was one of seven he would write. The letter represented a sure sign that Bomber Command regarded Oscar Furniss as killed in action. Smith, who had been piloting the aircraft that was first over the target on the Mailly raid, wrote:

> The loss of Flight Sergeant Furniss has deprived the Squadron of a Navigator of great promise whose characteristic skill and courage were an inspiration to us all, and on behalf of all members of the Squadron I should like to convey to you our very sincere sympathy.

He added that Oscar's personal effects had been carefully collected and forwarded to the RAF Central Depository. These were listed as: a photograph album, 26 negatives, 118 photos, a 1944 diary with no entry and two rolls of negatives (a full list of Oscar's possessions appears in Appendix 1). A week later Smith himself would be shot down during a night raid, saved only by the force of an explosion inside the aircraft itself which propelled him out of the blazing bomber. He was the only member of his crew to survive. The fragility of life was nowhere better illustrated than in the daily casualty lists emerging from Bomber Command.

Several weeks after the arrival of Squadron Leader Smith's personal missive, Oscar's final letter reached the family bearing news that can only have deepened their sadness. Oscar had written to his parents from his hospital bed at RAF Waddington where he battled his latest round of respiratory infections. He had been advised that the RAAF doctors now considered him medically unfit to continue as a member of Bomber Command and he was to be discharged and evacuated to Australia. Fate had been particularly unkind to the Furniss family. Oscar had been asked to fly two more missions while a replacement navigator was sought. He had flown three. That third mission was the raid on 3/4 May over Mailly-le-Camp. Bertha Furniss, now realising how close she had come to realising her long-held dream, can only have been devastated by this news.

On 6 September 1944 fate dealt the Furniss family a further blow with news that destroyed any hope that Oscar might have survived. RAAF Headquarters advised them that Oscar's fellow crew member Stan Jolly had not only managed to escape the burning aircraft, but had then evaded capture for several months in occupied France and had now arrived safely back in England. For Oscar and Bertha Furniss the joyful news of Stan's miraculous survival must have been bittersweet, coming as it did with confirmation that their son had certainly perished in the blaze.

Stan had relived the trauma of the crash in a vivid description of the last moments of the bomber. He told his RAF interviewers that, while he had heard Colin Dickson order the crew to abandon the aircraft, he had heard no acknowledgements from the crew members. Stan had seen just one other parachute and believed that this was possibly the flight engineer, Phil 'Taffy' Weaver. This could only confirm the Furniss family belief that Oscar had failed to escape from the aircraft. Yet, again, uncertainty was the byword as the RAAF could not confirm their son's death, nor could their sources clearly ascertain whether he had in fact survived and been taken prisoner by the Germans. This uncertainty was mirrored in the assertions of all the crew members' families who complained bitterly over the lack of information.

On 30 September the Furniss family must have been further unsettled by news from the Air Ministry that wireless operator Bob Hunter had also reached England and had been admitted to RAF Hospital Wroughton in Wiltshire where he was recovering from burns sustained during his escape from the blazing bomber. Again there was no sense that Oscar might have escaped the stricken aircraft or survived the crash. Indeed, in an interview with the RAF, Bob expressed his belief that the navigator — Oscar — and mid-upper gunner Horace 'Jack' Skellorn did not leave the aircraft. Bob also noted that the rear gunner, Hilton Forden, had possibly been hit by the enemy fighter as the rear turret was not rotated and his parachute remained hanging on its hook. Bob confirmed his belief that Nan had been flying at an altitude of between 5000 and 6000 feet when he jumped.

By the end of 1944 the Furniss family must have accepted that they would never see their son again. On 17 February 1945 the elder Oscar Furniss was notified by the Casualty Section that there was now no hope of finding Oscar alive. He responded with courtesy, expressing his appreciation for the condolences and messages of sympathy the family had received from members of the section. On 24 April 1945 the RAAF officially declared Oscar and the other missing crew members 'presumed dead'. The Furniss family was notified on 8 May 1945. The ugly process of requesting an official death certificate and claiming on Oscar's insurance policy then unfolded, a bureaucratic procedure that can only have compounded the family's grief.

As late as August 1945 when the war had been over for three months, Oscar's father was still corresponding over the vexed question of his son's personal effects. The loss of Oscar had clearly affected his health as he suffered a stroke later that month, remaining incapacitated into September 1945. He wrote again on 28 December 1945, addressing his enquiries to the Casualty Section and asking in particular about two cameras and a silver wing brooch. He added that an expensive wristwatch had also been sent to Oscar and should have arrived just prior to the date from which his son was posted as missing.

A reply on 7 January 1946 from the Central Repository advised that all possessions, excluding the wristwatch, had been itemised on Oscar's list of personal effects and would be returned to the family. Oscar and Bertha consoled themselves with the thought that the wristwatch would make its way home eventually. They were to be sorely disappointed. There is no record of the watch ever being recovered and it is possible that Oscar was wearing it at the time of the crash. It may have perished alongside him.

In a bizarre twist, on 19 March 1946, RAAF Overseas Headquarters in London wrote to No.2 MREU in France quoting Bob Hunter's belief that, while Oscar Furniss could not have escaped the aircraft, 'he was however safe and sound in it'. This was an extraordinary statement, particularly as Bob certainly saw Nan enveloped in flames and subsequently crash into a field. This may, however, have been the terminology used by the MI5 intelligence-gatherers who reviewed every interview and often conducted their own interviews with returned evaders. This phrase could only have meant that Oscar was 'secure' in the aircraft—in other words, that there was no way he could have escaped. Certainly German records stated unequivocally that two bodies had been recovered from the ruins of the bomber. Nan was recorded as shot down between midnight and 1.00am on 4 May 1944 with the remains of the aircrew retrieved and buried in the cemetery at 'Mers on Seine' (Méry-sur-Seine) on 7 May. The charred remnants of three aircrew had been recovered by local villagers from the smouldering wreckage of the bomber and buried in a common grave in the churchyard at Droupt-Sainte-Marie. Every man was now accounted for.

The sorry saga was finally closed on 5 April 1949 when the Department of Air advised Oscar and Bertha that the bodies of Oscar Furniss, Colin Dickson and Philip Weaver had been exhumed from their grave in the churchyard at Droupt-Sainte-Marie. However, it had not been possible to individually identify the men and they were consequently buried collectively, their grave marked with the names and service particulars of all three airmen.

For the elder Oscar Furniss, the trauma of losing his son must have been overwhelming. He suffered a second stroke in November-December 1947 and third stroke on 25 July 1949, two weeks after what would have been Oscar's 28th birthday. He died less than a week later, on 31 July 1949, just months after receiving the news of his son's final resting place. He was aged just 59. Bertha now shouldered the burden of her grief alone, her children sharing the task of caring for their stricken mother. Bertha's final missive from the Department of Air came on 27 April 1950 and enclosed a photograph of the wooden cross that marked Oscar's last resting place. Bertha would carry her deep sense of loss for the rest of her life and would visit Oscar's grave at Droupt-Sainte-Marie in the late 1950s with her eldest son, Frank.

Oscar, aged 21, and his older brother, Frank, at 71. These images provide some indication of how Oscar might have appeared in his later years had he survived (RAAF image, author image).

Oscar's medals: 1939–1945 Star with Bomber Command bar, Aircrew Europe Star, 1939–1945 Defence Medal, 1939–1945 War Medal, 1939-1945 Australian Service Medal (author image).

Colin Dickson. RAAF image

The Furniss family was by no means alone in their grief and the families of the other four aircrew who perished that night were likewise devastated by the news of their loss. As Heather Fisher, niece of Pilot Officer Colin Dickson, recounts:

> The loss of a healthy, exuberant son in his early twenties would be a blow to any family and in May 1944, this happened to my grandparents. Colin was their youngest child, born after Maurice, a serious and stern older son and Edna, their beloved daughter who was my mother. Edna and Col were the closest of siblings and collaborators in having fun. My mother often talked about parties and dances which she was only allowed to go to because Col would be there to look after her. He was

a fun-loving young man, keen on motor bikes and clever with electronics and mechanical repairs. War changed everything for this family in Kempsey. Colin enlisted in the RAAF and left for training while my mother married my father who was in the RAAF and they went off to Air Force bases in Victoria. When my mother received the news of Colin's death, she managed to travel by very irregular and unpredictable trains from Melbourne to Kempsey and back, with a small toddler and a baby, to be with my grandparents for a time. After the war my parents and my brother and I returned to Kempsey where my parents lived for the rest of their lives.

From an early age I was aware of Col as part of the family. He was talked about frequently and there was the photo of him on my grandparents' lounge room wall, smiling from the cockpit of 'Naughty Nan'. No doubt the presence of grandchildren enlivened my grandparents' lives and we had a lot of contact with them, often staying overnight. For many years we didn't understand the significance of the death of Col as he was often just a comfortable part of everyday conversation.

However, I later came to understand that my grandmother mourned him until she died. During the 1950s women had 'going out clothes' (a good dress or suit, hats, gloves, stockings and high-heeled shoes) to go anywhere in public—to church, to the shopping centre, to afternoon teas, to appointments, to social gatherings, etc—and on her outfit, my grandmother always wore an oval gold brooch with a safety chain attached, pinned to her dress or jacket lapel. This brooch opened like a locket and had Col's photo inside. I am sure my grandfather mourned as well but in a different way—this loving, quiet, gentle man never mentioned Col. Years after my grandparents' deaths, a small street in East Kempsey was named Colin Dickson Street.

To have had contact with the survivors of Colin's RAAF crew was a most remarkable and deeply affecting event in my mother's later life. It must have been a common feeling when their loved one died in a distant land, that this part of their family would soon be forgotten by the world at large.

Colin Dickson Street, East Kempsey (image courtesy of Helen Edmunds).

Philip 'Taffy' Weaver (image courtesy of the Weaver family via Llansamlet Historical Society).

Colin Weaver, nephew of Sergeant Philip 'Taffy' Weaver, describes the impact of the death of his uncle, an event that clearly traumatised his family:

Welsh people are only ever known within their family by their given name. It is the Australians who always seem to find a nickname for their friends and foe alike. Phil was known by his Aussie crew mates and most others outside Wales by the default name for the Welsh, 'Taffy' or 'Taff', after the River Taff in Cardiff.

His father, William, laboured as a tube worker at the furnace of the local steel works. This is one of the dirtiest jobs in one of the hottest areas of steel making. The job was better paid than most labouring jobs. It meant that Phil's parents could afford an education for him while most of the boys he grew up with would have been working by age 12.

While Philip was employed by the local gas authority in a clerical role his understanding of mechanical operations was a factor in his chosen RAFVR [RAF Volunteer Reserve] career. A diligent note-taker during his RAF training as a flight engineer, Phil quickly grasped the tasks before him. The family still has his engineering notebook from that training.

Tragedy followed Philip as he matured into his early 30s. He joined the RAFVR as his way of dealing with a broken long-term relationship. His loss in France was the final tragedy. For his parents, the loss of their son was a bitter pill to swallow. They were in their 60s and this was the second son they had lost, Phil's younger brother Alfred had died in 1925 aged three.

Phil's parents, brothers and sisters never got over the loss. His parents visited the gravesite of their son, interred in a common grave with Col Dickson and Oscar Furniss, in the churchyard at Droupt-Sainte-Marie in the 1950s to say their final goodbyes to their beloved son.

Sergeant Horace 'Jack' Skellorn was also deeply missed by his family, as his sister-in-law, Lorna Skellorn, writes. While she never knew Horace, she 'lives with him every day' through her husband Keith, Horace's brother:

Photographs of Horace and his brother Keith (now aged in his eighties) show how Horace might have looked in his senior years (images courtesy of the Skellorn family).

Horace was the eldest son of John and Martha Skellorn of Ashtonunder-Lyne, Lancashire. His younger siblings were Frank, who died as an infant, and Keith. Keith was 10 years younger than Horace. His parents were recognised as down-to-earth, honest working-class folk. His dad, John, worked in the local cotton mills.

> I married Keith in 1963 so I never knew Horace, yet I feel that I do know him by the loving way he was spoken of by the family. He was loved very much and deeply missed by his parents. Horace's mother often spoke of her missing son, his father not so often.
>
> Horace was the 'big brother in uniform' hero to Keith. Some 72 years later Keith still struggles to mention Horace's name without a tear in his eye. When Horace came home on leave he would take Keith to a local café for a treat; a nine-year-old boy walking around town with his RAF uniformed brother.
>
> Horace formed a very strong bond with the rest of his crew. They were his mates and he spoke constantly of them while he was at home. The five Australians in the crew were clearly a strong influence on Horace; 'when the war was ended he wasn't staying in England, he was off to Australia'.

John Skellorn was quite proud that his eldest son didn't have much respect for the British officers or upper class. When Keith was called up to do his National Service he wanted to be in the RAF like his big brother. Keith was discharged after three days on medical grounds. John Skellorn then wrote to the RAF telling them 'they had already taken one son and were not getting another'.

When Horace visited home on short leave breaks he would always give his mother a goodbye kiss and a hug on the front step before walking down the path to the front gate. On what was to be his last visit home he had said his goodbyes and walked to the gate; then he turned and went back to his mother and gave her a heartfelt hug and a kiss and said he loved her. The family have felt to this day that Horace knew it would be his last visit home.

Hilton Forden RAAF image

Flight Sergeant Hilton Forden's father wrote a series of heartfelt letters which remained on Hilton's casualty file. The impact of his death on his family is immediately obvious from the rawness of the letters. George Forden, Hilton's father, served with the 1st Australian General Hospital during World War I. George had witnessed the extraordinary survival skills of young Australian servicemen and the durability of the human body in extremely adverse circumstances. He struggled to accept that his son was missing and refused to acknowledge the possibility that Hilton's life might have been taken by an attacking enemy fighter. Some 12 months after the mission and motivated by the intelligence reports of Stan Jolly and Bob Hunter,

George wrote to Squadron Leader J.D. Robertshaw and the RAF Dominion Air Force Missing Research and Inquiry Service searching for some glimmer of hope that his son might have survived:

> Knowing that [Stan] Jolly was cared for by local inhabitants for a 4 month period before being liberated, if the aircraft was destroyed in this area it is strange that there is no debris or perhaps it managed to proceed towards the French coast and fell in territory only just released from enemy control. [Bob] Hunter says that my son, Hilton Hardcastle Forden, was possibly hit and there is reason to believe may be suffering from loss of memory. He is only 21 now and has a young fresh complexion. He may be cared for by an old lady in the forest and may not know his identity.
>
> Our long suspense makes us very grateful for any help.
>
> George J Forden
>
> 14th May 1945

It would be another four years before Horace's remains were exhumed from his grave in Saint-Remy-sous-Barbuise and his identity confirmed from his dog tags. For many years after the war, George sent money to the Hunter and Jolly families at Christmas so that they could buy presents for their children and also occasionally visited them. Hilton had a sister Cynthia who died from multiple sclerosis in 1962. George Forden was 55 when he lost his son and, following the loss of his daughter, he lived out his final years as a lonely man with a heavy and grieving heart.

Bob Hunter (image courtesy of the Hunter family).

In spite of the gravity of Flight Sergeant Bob Hunter's wounds, he recovered sufficiently to lead a relatively normal life after the war. While his death was ultimately ascribed in no small part to these wounds, the life he lived was characterised by his significant contribution to his community. His family later described the impact of his wounds on his daily life:

> Our dad, Bob Hunter, was a loving husband and father, tireless community worker and compassionate friend. Dad had

a great sense of humour, and a belief in social justice and equity. His war service played a big part in his life, and impacted on that of his family when we were growing up. Dad's injuries were plain to see in his scarred and deformed hands, but he almost never talked about his experiences in the war. Even though his hands were severely scarred, many people knew him for years and never noticed them. He was a strong character who wasn't defined by his injuries or misfortunes. He lived a full and productive life, although he was a lifelong insomniac. He made the most beautiful cedar furniture, meticulously French polished, to furnish our house in the 60s. When Dad died, he was the secretary of the Pittsworth High School P&C, secretary of the Pittsworth Bowls Club and incoming president of the Pittsworth Rotary Club. If there was a working bee, you could count on him being there.

There were numerous times in our youth when he would be admitted to Repatriation General Hospital, Greenslopes, in Brisbane. While he was there, he always showed friendship and compassion to the older WWI veterans who comprised the bulk of the men in the wards. When he was admitted to Greenslopes after a stroke in August 1972, Janet visited him every day, and witnessed the love and friendship offered to him by the old diggers as he voluntarily took the tea trolley around the ward every morning, chatting to each and every one of them on his way. Of course this helped Dad in his recuperation as well. He always seemed to be the youngest person in there.

Our family always kept in touch with the family of the French Nurse, Genevieve (Jenny) Lamy (née Daviou), who saved Dad's life by nursing him for three days around the clock when he was first brought into the hospital in Troyes, badly burnt and with little hope of survival. Her father was one of the surgeons who operated on Dad's hands, and Jenny's mother went into the operating theatre to argue that Dad's hands should not be amputated. The doctors' response was that he would not survive otherwise. She replied 'He's only 21. What will he do without his hands for the rest of his life?' She said she would prefer him not to survive were that to be the case. When Dad became conscious after the surgery, he looked at the length of his bandages and thought with relief, 'I've still got my hands!' How lucky he was to have a woman of such character to advocate for him in his deepest hour of need.

As children, we often looked at the photograph of the young men in the crew of Dad's plane when it was shot down, and we always thought of their families, even though we didn't know them all. We met Mr Forden, Hilton Forden's father, on several occasions, and I think it gave him some comfort to meet both us and the Jolly children, and to think what might have been had his son survived. Dad and Stan Jolly were lifelong friends, but there was always a deep respect felt by all of us for the families of Dad's crew members who didn't manage to escape from the plane. To the families of those brave men, we pass on our deepest condolences. Although it happened over 70 years ago, we know these men are still remembered with a love that burns as strongly as it did all those years ago.

We, the children of Bob Hunter, remember Dad with love, pride and affection. Our mother, Barbara, loved him to her dying day, having been widowed at 41 years of age. She said at her 80th birthday party, that her whole world collapsed when she lost him.

Flight Sergeant, later Warrant Officer Stan Jolly as a RAAF Cadet in 1942 and as a retired businessman in 1995 (images courtesy of the Jolly family).

The happiest day in the life of the young Phyllis Corbet was Wednesday 6 September 1944, the day she received a cable which read: 'Gave Hitler the flick'. It was from her fiancé Stan who had being missing in action for four months and for whom her heart and mind wrestled between the reality that he may have been killed in action and the hope that he was alive and safely hidden somewhere. With the liberation of the area in which Stan had been hiding, he was safely delivered to Allied forces and was promptly transported from Utah beach to Weymouth overnight in a flat-bottomed landing craft. His first action once back on British soil was to cable his fiancée and parents. Then followed a protracted round of intelligence interviews and reminiscing with Bob Hunter who he met a week after his return. Having visited his squadron, Stan sailed from the UK on 25 October 1944 aboard the *Mauretania,* heading for New York in a west-bound crossing nursing entirely different emotions to those of his east-bound crossing 15 months earlier. Amid the daily round of gunnery practice and submarine watch which reminded him that the war continued, at least in this part of the world, Stan pondered the fact that a great deal had been crammed into those last 15 months.

Stan left San Francisco for the Pacific crossing aboard the *Lurline,* describing his position on the ship as 'deck cargo', but grateful to be heading home at last. He finally caught sight of his beloved Glass House Mountains, rising dramatically in the hinterland north of Brisbane, in the breaking day of 16 January 1945. The *Lurline* docked in Brisbane at 10.56am. Two weeks later, Stan and Phyllis were married. Stan returned to his old job as a salesman at Finney Isles, now David Jones, in Brisbane following his discharge from the RAAF on 19 October 1945. Stan and Phyllis had three children and eight grandchildren. Stan retired in 1983 and passed away on 12 August 2001. At the time of writing Phyllis still lives in their family home.

| | | |
|---|---|---|
| A.422038 | Pilot Officer | Dickson, C. |
| A.423700 | Flight Sergeant | Furniss, O.S. |
| 1836169 | Sergeant | Weaver, P.J. |
| 2209827 | Sergeant | Skellorn, H. |
| A.424403 | Flight Sergeant | Forden, H.H. |

The 5 Group Roll of Honour and the names of Naughty Nan's crew. The roll is held in the Airmen's Chapel at Lincoln Cathedral (author images).

The enormous losses in Bomber Command ensured that the raw grief of loss experienced by these families applied also to thousands of families who lost husbands, fathers, sons, brothers and cherished relatives during the war. A total of 125,000 airmen served in Bomber Command during World War II, with 55,000 losing their lives, including 7000 in training accidents. Some 10,000 Australians served in Bomber Command of whom 3486 never returned home. Thousands who did carried permanent scars, both physical and mental.

# CHAPTER 13

# COMMEMORATING THE LOST CREW

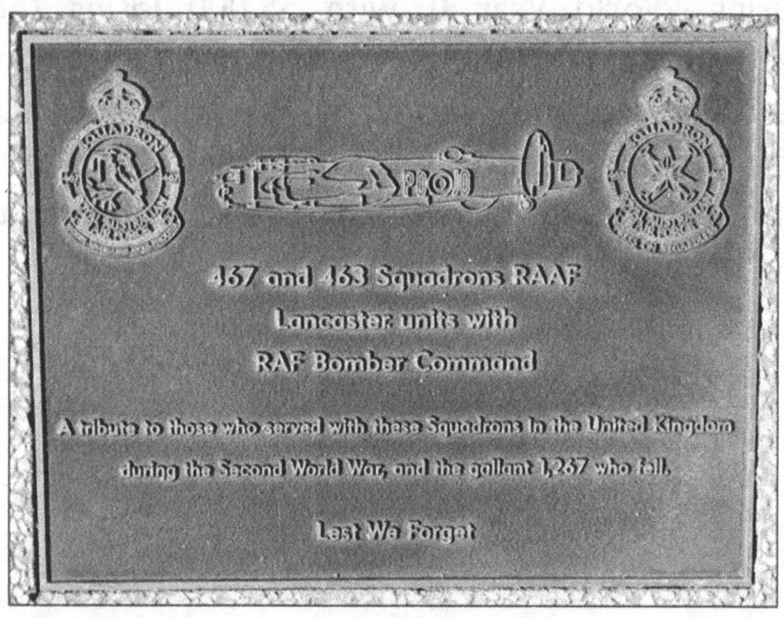


Commemorative plaque in honour of 467 and 463 squadrons in the grounds of the Australian War Memorial in Canberra (author image).

Given the way Naughty Nan is presumed to have broken up on impact, the bodies of the crew members were initially discovered in two separate locations and were consequently buried in two graves 19 kilometres apart. The three crew in the front of Nan—Colin Dickson, Philip

Weaver and Oscar Furniss—were buried in the churchyard at Droupt-Sainte-Marie. The two gunners — Hilton Forden and Horace Skellorn — were interred in Saint-Remy-sous-Barbuise. According to local folklore, in the minutes immediately following the crash, the local villagers dashed to the site hoping to rescue any surviving airmen. However the Germans had beaten them to both the damaged tail section and the smouldering wreck and kept the villagers at bay. The locals watched as the Germans loaded what appeared to be one or two bodies onto a truck and drove them away. The following morning the villagers attempted once again to reach the site and this time they succeeded. While sections of the wreck were still smouldering, they managed to retrieve the charred remains of three airmen and buried them in a single coffin in the local churchyard. The fire had done its job: the total weight of the charred remains amounted to just five kilograms. On the grave the villagers erected a sign which read: *Ici reposent les restes d'aviateurs morts pour la liberation le 4 Mai 1944* ('Here lie the remains of airmen who died for the liberation [of France] on 4 May 1944').

When all the bodies were exhumed in 1949 to confirm their identity, the MREU team recorded that these three bodies could not be individually identified. However those uncovered at Saint-Remy were certainly identifiable—Hilton Forden by his dog tags and Horace Skellorn by his RAF uniform. That these dog tags and uniform were not charred beyond recognition suggests that the section of the aircraft in which the men sat had separated from the burning front half before or on final impact. The section that Stan Jolly saw fall away could have been the rear section of the fuselage containing the two gunners—although it could also have been the burning left wing.

The first grave marker was replaced by a wooden cross and then a headstone. In March 1983 the remains of the airmen buried in the churchyard at Droupt-Saint-Marie were again exhumed to be interred in the Commonwealth War Graves Commission Terlincthun Cemetery close to the town of Wimille.

The first official wooden grave marker at Droupt-Sainte-Marie showing the incorrect rank for Colin

Dickson (MREU). Replacement headstone at Droupt-Sainte-Marie (author image).

Two grave plots in the churchyard. The three crew of Naughty Nan are in the single plot at the rear (author image).

The second grave of three headstones marks the final resting place of the crew of Lancaster DV374 of 463 Squadron, RAAF, which was shot down before reaching its target on 19 July 1944. The four graves were later exhumed and the remains moved to the Commonwealth War Graves Terlincthun Cemetery at Wimille.

Equipage de Lancaster JA901
467 SQN RAAF

| | | | |
|---|---|---|---|
| Plt Off | C. DICKSON | RAAF | Pilot |
| F Sgt | H. FORDEN | RAAF | Air Gnr |
| F Sgt | D. FURNISS | RAAF | Nav |
| Sgt | H. SKELLORN | RAF | Air Gnr |
| Sgt | P. WEAVER | RAF | Flt Eng |

*Morts le 4 Mai 1944*

The obelisk and plaque in the churchyard at Droupt-Sainte-Marie (author images).

With the move to Terlincthun, an elegant obelisk was erected in the front of the churchyard in memory of the airmen (a process that saw the O in Oscar's name become a D, an error that has taken over 30 years to correct). The local townspeople were determined never to forget the sacrifice of these courageous young men.

C. DICKSON

The headstone on the grave (nearest to camera) at Terlincthun (author images).

An obelisk was also erected in Wentworth Falls, originally at the intersection of Station Street with the Great Western Highway. It was later moved to a site opposite the railway station. Oscar's family home sits close by, on the right-hand end of the building in the background—he has finally come home (author images).

Phil 'Taffy' Weaver is remembered on the War Memorial in Primrose Park in his home town of Llansamlet, Wales (image courtesy of Llansamlet Historical Society).

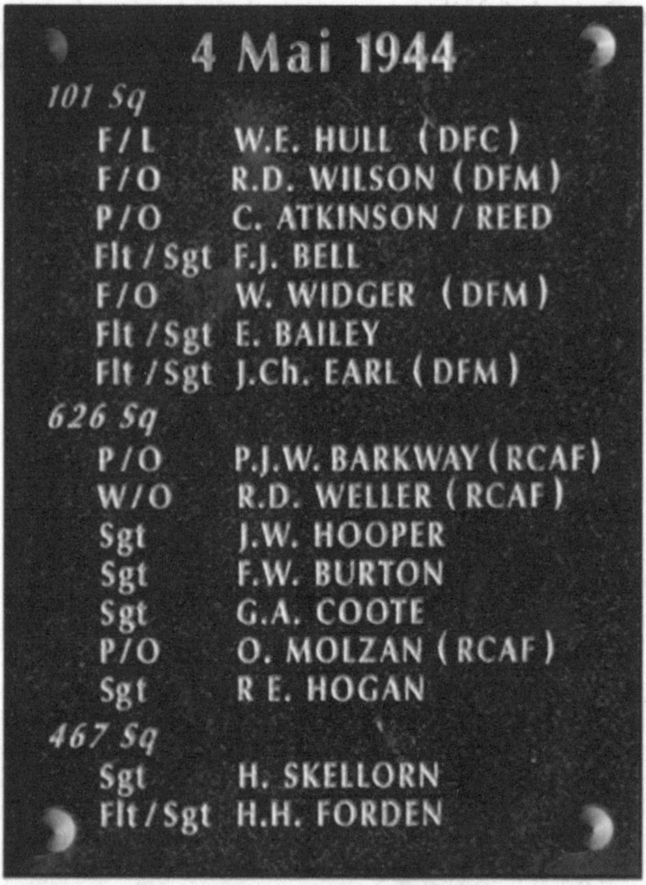

4 Mai 1944

*101 Sq*

F/L W.E. HULL (DFC)
F/O R.D. WILSON (DFM)
P/O C. ATKINSON / REED
Flt / Sgt F.J. BELL
F/O W. WIDGER (DFM)
Flt / Sgt E. BAILEY
Flt / Sgt J.Ch. EARL (DFM)

*626 Sq*

P/O P.J.W. BARKWAY (RCAF)
W/O R.D. WELLER (RCAF)
Sgt J.W. HOOPER
Sgt F.W. BURTON
Sgt G.A. COOTE
P/O O. MOLZAN (RCAF)
Sgt R E. HOGAN

*467 Sq*

Sgt H. SKELLORN
Flt/Sgt H.H. FORDEN

The bodies of Horace Skellorn and Hilton Forden were buried at Saint-Remy-sous-Barbuise with the crews of two other bombers lost on the Mailly raid (Claude Dannau image).

The true epitaph to this story comes from the people of Mailly-le-Camp who, for many years have held a commemorative service at the barracks to remember the sacrifice of 258 brave airmen on 3/4 May 1944. Organised by the French *l'Association Mailly 3/4 Mai 1944,* the first service was held in drizzling rain in 1991 and led by Group Captain Leonard Cheshire, then Baron Cheshire, VC, OM, DSO and two bars, DFC, who was the Master Bomber on the night of the raid. The association was formed with the visit of the brother of a RAF navigator from 101 Squadron who had been killed nearby. The Mailly memorial, featuring a stylised 'M' in masonry and a damaged Lancaster propeller blade, was erected in the grounds of the rebuilt Mailly barracks.

The Mailly memorial.

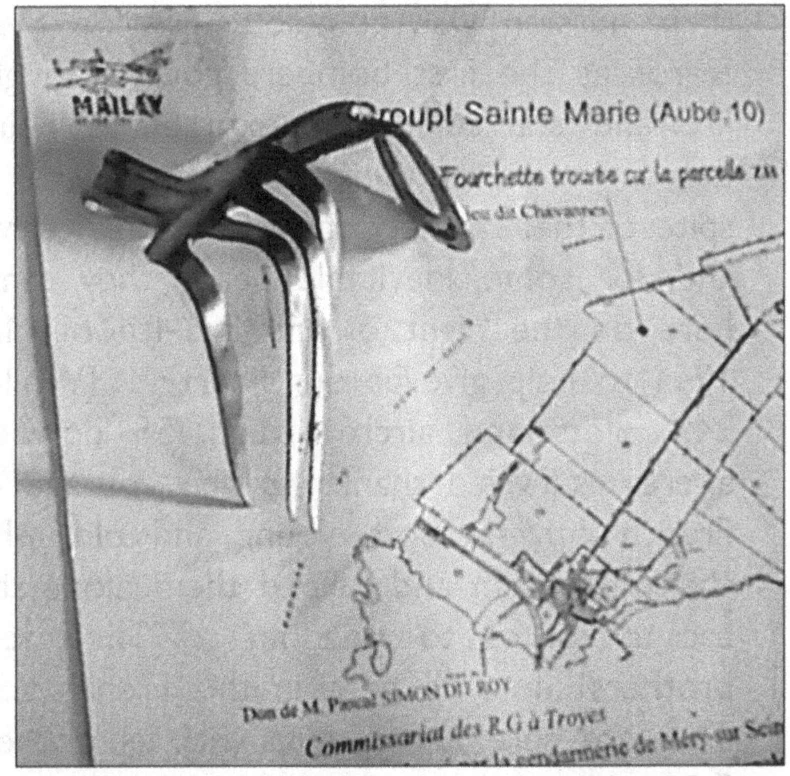


A small relic from Naughty Nan—a fork found in the wreckage of the aircraft is held in the village community centre. Pieces of the fuselage are also held by the families of the survivors (author images).

In the words of Monsieur Francois Meunier, a past president of the Mailly Association:

> These young men from the United Kingdom, from Canada, from Australia and from New Zealand, on [the] clear night of the 3rd/4th of May 1944, anxious and tense from the outset, serving on yet another mission, becoming more nervous when the attack did not go to plan, persevered until

> their mission was complete. Imagine their terror as the first bombers got hit, caught fire and started their inexorable spinning descent towards their tragic destiny ... In spite of their anxiety, their fear, their terror and, for some, inevitable death, they came here on the night of the 3rd/4th of May 1944 to help give us our liberty ... [While] 249 pilots and aircrew died, 55 downed aircrew survived thanks to the courage of French citizens, both young and old, who sheltered them and helped them along the escape routes to freedom ... [Their lost brothers] now lie here in this French soil. They are here, amongst us, with us, in their flying suits and boots, to give us once again a fraternal smile. They remind us of the price they have paid for our liberty.[41]

The late David Collins, writing for *Dispersal,* the quarterly magazine of the Newark Air Museum, penned a moving account of the visit to France of the last surviving member of Naughty Nan's aircrew:

> In 1994, Stan Jolly, accompanied by Phyllis, his wife of 50 years, returned to France to find his rescuers and thank them. Instead he found a people still grateful for what he and all the other Allied airmen had done to liberate their country. That

> gratitude, movingly, was put into words on VE Day 1994 by the Mayor of Chapelle-Vallon in a short but heartfelt speech he made over the graves of the airmen killed in the Mailly raid. 'To the men buried here, I would like to tell you this. No, you were not unlucky adventurers, flying that night in the sky of France, but heroic combatants, brothers-in-arms of French soldiers. You came here to help them recover the ground of France and allow her to regain her identity, her independence, and her freedom. You lost your lives to give us freedom, we cannot thank you enough.'[42]

The crew of Naughty Nan now rest in peace as honoured brothers-in-arms of all who died to liberate France. From Colin Dickson, the pilot from East Kempsey, Horace Skellorn, the lad from Lancashire, Hilton Forden, the young clerk from Newcastle, Philip Weaver from the pretty Welsh town of Llansamlet, to Oscar Furniss, the boy from Wentworth Falls, they will never be forgotten.

Sculpture of the seven crew members of a Lancaster bomber in London that pays tribute to the enormous contribution and sacrifice of the bomber crews during World War II.

The Airmen's Memorial opposite Hyde Park Gate, London (author images).

# APPENDIX I

# LIST OF OSCAR'S PERSONAL EFFECTS

I carton
I leather wallet containing:
I suitcase (damaged)
I steel mirror
I pr ice skating boots
I notebook
I pr galoshes souvenir cards
I 620 Brownie camera
I driver's licence
I Bantam Kodak camera
I fountain pen (less top)
2 cycle lamps F&R
I Blackbird fountain pen
3 D bars
2 sets Sgts chevrons
3 pipes
2 N badges *
2 pks playing cards
I fork
2 torch cases
I spoon
3 leather straps

1 padlock
1 leather purse
1 box marking equipment
2 leather cigarette cases
5 booklets
1 metal cigarette case
1 black leather satchel (loose leaf)
1 fabric cigarette case (crested)
1 match container
1 1944 diary (no entry)
2 LAC badges
58 souvenir coins
1 Australian soldiers pocket book
1 leather money belt
2 pkts photo corners
1 paint brush
1 programme
1 tobacco pouch
1 motor cycle driver's licence
1 pr nail clippers
1 pkt postcards and viewers
1 tooth brush
5 black ties
1 bottle opener
2 pr leather gloves
1 eye shield
1 pr swim trunks
1 pennant *
1 polishing pad

2 pkts sensitised paper
37 sox
1 paper knife
3 balaclavas
1 dog mascot
1 Cranwell front
1 metal buffalo *
1 pr wool gloves
2 safety razors in tin
2 wool scarves
1 pr spectacles in case
2 wool pullovers
1 metal N broach
1 pr sheepskin mittens
1 comb
7 singlets
1 spanner
2 shirts
1 pr suspenders
4 pr draws
1 book mark
18 handkerchiefs
1 metal crown*
2 pr ladies silk stockings
3 O badges *
1 universal kit bag
1 album of photos
2 suits pyjamas
1 pkt negatives

1 pk of airgraph letters
1 pkt photos
2 rolls of negatives.

The items marked * are still with the family.

There was no further record of the wristwatch; it is possible Oscar had received it and was wearing it on the Mailly mission. Oscar's last letter to his family was written following his discharge from hospital on 29 April.

# APPENDIX 2

# STAN JOLLY'S STORY

## —TRAIN RIDE TO THE DEVIL'S DEN

Stan Jolly's story of evasion following the crash of the Naughty Nan was sourced by the late David Collins and published in *Dispersal*, August–November 2007. The explanatory comments (written in italics) come from several sources including 'My Air Force Experience', Stan's unpublished private autobiography which was written in 1988 and updated by his children after his passing.

It had all started routinely enough, if being sent to bomb a Panzer division just outside the village of Mailly-le-Camp 70 kilometres south of Rheims could be said to be 'routine'. But from the moment his Lancaster bomber arrived over the target, with the son of Brisbane's original Lord Mayor William Jolly, perched in his bomb aimer's position in the nose of the aircraft, 'routine' procedure started bending out of all recognition. Instead of making the customary quick pass over the target, the Lancasters of 467 Squadron were instructed not to drop their bombs but to stooge around and await further orders. At the time an anxious Stan Jolly fretted that the Pathfinders were late in marking the target, but years later he learned that one of the delays was caused by the bombing leader's faulty radio. Whatever the reason, by the time his plane ('Naughty Nan' as her crew had christened her) eventually dropped her bombs on the massed German armour below, the sky over Mailly was swarming with *Luftwaffe* fighters. Of the 362 heavy bombers that started out on the raid, 42 would never return to base, Naughty Nan among them! Stan never saw the fighter which shot his plane down. Even when he heard the sound of bullets striking metal, he still did not realise that his 'routine' was about to be broken. It didn't help that skipper Colin Dickson used an almost conversational tone when he gave the order for the crew to bail out [sic]. It was not until he heard Dickson instruct the flight engineer to 'feather the props' that it sank in that their situation was perilous. One wing was blazing furiously. The plane was going down! He had never made a parachute jump in his life. Indeed his only training in this regard involved jumping off a 30-centimetre box and rolling onto his side, hardly a realistic simulation of a 5000-foot drop through a night sky into enemy-occupied France.

*At 5000 feet Naughty Nan was in the lowest wave of bombers over the target and the crew was concerned about being hit by the bombs of the aircraft above as had almost occurred five nights earlier on the raid to Bordeaux.*

Still, once the order was given Stan didn't hang around for a debate and immediately plunged through the escape hatch which was located conveniently beneath his post.

*Getting out of the aircraft wasn't that simple. When Stan first tried to open the hatch it wouldn't budge. The procedure was to open it and force it away to one side but the air pressure was against him. He finally got it open only for the hatch to be blown back and jam upright in its frame. Stan eventually pushed the recalcitrant hatch far enough to one side to slide down and out of the hole. Stan had been aware of the boots and person of Taffy Weaver standing behind him while he struggled with the hatch. Once clear of the burning aircraft Stan finally saw only one other parachute and that was below him. This puzzled Stan as he couldn't understand how Taffy, who was behind him in Naughty Nan, could now be below him. It was four months later that Stan learnt who was wearing the other parachute.*

Barely had his parachute opened when the doomed Lancaster exploded into a ball of fire.

*Naughty Nan tumbled to the left and went nose first into the ground around 1.4 kilometres north-east of Droupt-Sainte-Marie. A burning section broke off on impact.*

Desperately, he searched for other 'chutes but could spot only one away in the distance, that of wireless operator Bob Hunter. The other five crew members were dead! Guessing that the Germans must have seen his parachute and would expect him to head south towards neutral Spain, Stan struck out east, anxious to put as much distance between him and the crash site before morning. After catching a few hours of fitful sleep in a forest, he pushed on the next day [Thursday 4 May] but by mid-afternoon, thirst had got the better of adrenalin. Spying a church steeple [*which he later identified as in the village of Saint-Remy-sous-Barbuise*] he crept up to the village of Villacerf, but decided to hole up in a small quarry until darkness provided cover enough to find a drink. Scarcely had he settled in for the wait than two young French girls wandered into the quarry to play and a startled Stan Jolly could do nothing more than place his forefinger across his lips and pleadingly say 'Sssshh'. Thankfully some things are the same in all languages and the older girl, Odette Berque, nodded and silently rushed off to summon her father who was ploughing nearby. Using a language card from his escape kit, Stan explained his predicament to the man who in turn summoned his wife, Madame Berque. Stan wasn't quite certain what to expect from this impressive-looking middle-aged woman, but he certainly wasn't prepared for the flurry of kisses and hugs which she showered on him. [*Madame Berque also brought Stan a double-breasted suit for him to change into before he was led to their home. Stan was still wearing his RAAF shoes.*]

That night, safe in the Berque cottage, he outlined his plan to walk to Spain. 'Non, Non,' they insisted and haltingly made him understand that he would encounter too many Germans on that route. Far wiser, they said, to continue east to Paris [*actually to the north-west of where they were*] in the hope of picking up a southbound train. Next morning, accompanied by the intrepid Madame Berque, he set off for the nearby railway station at Payns, where she bought him a ticket for Paris using 100 francs from his escape kit's cache to pay the fare. Then, whispering a fervent 'au revoir', she turned and left him. Stan fancied he could see the relief on her face as she said goodbye, but years later he would learn that this extraordinary Frenchwoman had far more to worry about than a single Allied airman. Throughout the war she gave shelter to a group of Jewish children, a crime punishable by death. For the moment however, Stan Jolly had problems of his own. As his Paris-bound train pulled into the next station, Romilly-sur-Seine, he noticed a platoon of [German] soldiers waiting on the platform. Thankfully, they wanted nothing more than to commandeer his carriage. But after moving to the next carriage, Stan discovered the only untaken seat was directly opposite a German soldier! Realising that it would be more conspicuous to stand there than to brazen it out, he nervously sat down, stretching like a contortionist as he simultaneously tried to cover up both his RAAF polo-neck jumper and his 'escaper' flying boots which he had cut down to shoe size. He had done a rough and ready job with his pocket knife and he was convinced the German could not help but notice the incriminating tufts of wool still sticking out of his crudely converted boots.

*Most of the compass directions mentioned in the text don't match the map—Stan was using a compass the size of a button in less than ideal conditions. He still thought he would strike out for Spain once he reached Paris.*

Given time, the daydreaming German soldier might have spotted the flaws in his disguise but an observant French couple who had boarded the train with Stan at Payns didn't give the German the chance. Although they had said nothing, they had clearly deduced that their fidgety travelling companion was an Allied evader and, as soon as a seat became available, they tapped him on the shoulder and motioned for him to join them. Then, like the hot potato that he was, they passed him on to a railway guard in Paris and, unwittingly, into the safe hands of the French Underground. 'A young man's beer is almost one of the rites of passage'—in Stan Jolly's case it could have easily qualified him for the last rites! As a RAAF evader on the run in France after being shot down during a bombing raid, Stan had confided his identity to a seemingly friendly railway guard at the Gare de l'Est station in Paris. The guard's eyes lit up when he heard the whispered word 'parachutist' and he motioned for the young Australian to follow him. Realising it was now a case of 'in for a penny, in for a pound', Stan complied. Heavy doors swung open and suddenly Stan found himself surrounded by hundreds of Germans, *Wehrmacht, Luftwaffe,* and *Kriegsmarine,* none of whom, thankfully, showed the least interest in the flimsily disguised airman. Panic stricken, Stan almost turned and fled, but the ever-smiling railway guard motioned him forward through the crush to the public bar. The brazen Frenchman wanted nothing more than to buy an Allied airman a drink and, Germans or no Germans, he was not to be denied the privilege. All of this put Stan

Jolly in something of a fix. A teetotaller at the time, he would have gladly settled for a lemonade; but having no idea how to explain himself in French, he summoned up his best Gallic accent and brusquely ordered 'un biere' Given the week he had endured, a stiff calming rum might perhaps have been more appropriate. Stan Jolly never did reach sunny Spain. Shunted from house to house by the Underground, he was still in Paris when the Allied forces hit the Normandy beaches on D-Day, 6 June. At that point the BBC broadcast instructions for all Allied evaders to sit tight and await liberation. Yet Stan was almost brought undone when his excited hosts decided the Germans had pulled out of the suburb of Villemomble [14 kilometres east of Paris] and paraded him as a guest of honour at a wild celebration at the local town hall—only for them all to scatter when the Germans returned, spraying bullets and not champagne. It was only another week before the party was in full swing again, this time for real after the liberation of Paris on 26 August.

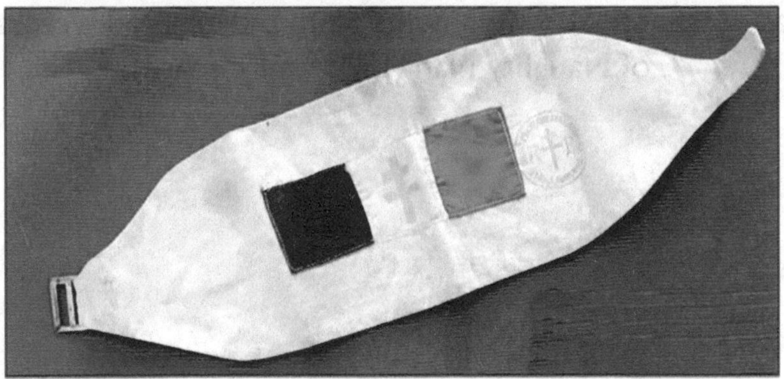

The French Forces of the Interior (FFI) provided Stan a French identification card dated 12 March 1943 and a FFI armband (Jolly family images).

During Stan and his wife Phyllis' visit to Mailly in 1994, he was presented with fragments from the charred wreckage of Naughty Nan (Jolly family image).

The Gare de l'Est where Stan shared a beer in a bar full of German soldiers following his train trip from Payns (author image).

# APPENDIX 3

# BOB HUNTER'S STORY

## –WALKING TO RESCUE AND HOSPITAL

This account is based on an article by the late David Collins published in the November 2007 issue of *Dispersal,* the quarterly magazine of the Newark Air Museum. Clarifying information from the Hunter family and other sources has been added as necessary in italics. The account is taken from the diary of Bob Hunter, written in September-October 1944, five months after his liberation and return to England. Additional information supplied by Bob's wife, Barbara, appears in italics.

We had some trouble before reaching the target, at times it was chaotic with different messages coming over the wireless. We could see aircraft going down in flames. We eventually dropped our bomb load on the target ... and a few moments later we were attacked, Naughty Nan shook like a tree in a wind storm. Colin, the skipper immediately shouted 'OK fellers, bale out, feather 'em Taff, feather 'em Taff!' Perhaps the last words he ever spoke. Our port motors were on fire and the petrol tanks in the port wing were blazing fiercely. I grabbed my parachute and bashed it onto the hooks of my harness, pulled off my helmet and moved into Oscar's compartment, Oscar had his 'chute on but wasn't moving, and I could see that he wouldn't move again, he had lost his nerve.

I knew that it would be of no use to wait for him, so I turned to make my exit through the rear fuselage door. I hurdled through the space above the main spar. From here to the tail our kite was blazing. The aluminium fuselage, the oil from the gun turrets pipeline had burst, everything seemed to be burning. I thought of turning and again making my way to the front hatch where there appeared to be no flames, however I took the fire to be the lesser of two evils and I have since proved it to be correct. All these scenes and thoughts impressed themselves on my mind in a second or so before I placed my right hand over my eyes and ran into the flames. I was bent over almost double with my body more or less protecting my 'chute from the flames, I could feel and hear the explosions from the ammunition in the machine-gun belt to the rear turret. I believe I was hit in the leg by a red hot case as I had a burn over half an inch deep in my right leg. On reaching the rear door I grasped the knob with my left hand which was already very badly burned. The door refused to open and while struggling with it my left foot pierced the floor and I fell. The floor gave way and the lower part of my body was completely out of the aircraft. The wind stream caught me and turned me round in the opposite direction to that in which I fell. By this time I was completely exhausted and had given up all hope. I attempted to get through the hole in the floor, but my 'chute would not go through. At this moment a thought raced through my mind, I thought of my mother and how would she take it if I were to die, this seemed to give me more strength for a final effort. I gave a lunge with my feet and found myself on my hands and knees. I merely touched the door, it opened, and I crawled over the step. I was free of the flames and was turning over and over as I fell. I clutched and clutched at the D handle of my 'chute, perhaps a dozen times before it opened. Even now I have no remembrance or sensation of pulling the cord, but my 'chute finally opened and I was making my descent. I fell into a plantation of fir trees and was not touched by a single twig. The 'chute came down over the top of a tree and broke my fall, so that my feet were barely on the ground. I looked at my hands, imagining my right hand to be the more badly burned (the skin had peeled off from the palm of my hand and was hanging down attached to my hand by small pieces of skin on the first and little fingers). I released my harness with my left hand, which today still bears the result in missing flesh and scars. The lower part of my body was completely naked from my 'Mae West' down to my flying boots which were covered with small particles of molten metal.

After this I began walking till I came to a small village [identified in the discussion at the end of this appendix] perhaps two to three hours later. I tried every house in this village, but no-one would assist me. I finally crept around to the rear door of one house and opened the door with my shoulder and I was allowed to stay there. The pain from my hands was intense and after pacing the floor for several hours the French Resistance or FFI came for me. I was placed on a stretcher and carried a long distance to their headquarters, about a two-hour trip. About midday the next day[4 May] a utility truck came and I then met a Flying Officer Neville Mutter of 65 Squadron, Typhoons, who had been shot down the previous day. While I was in hospital I received letters from him till he began his journey back to our line in Normandy. I was placed in this truck and taken through the city which I later found to be Troyes. I was taken to a house in the suburbs and remained till sometime after dark. By this time my hands were a tremendous size, and Dad's wedding ring was cut from my finger with a dirty pair of clippers. The ring was covered in burnt flesh, but I had no feeling of pain as by this time circulation had stopped in my hands and they were quite dead. During my short stay at this home, the neighbours were invited in to see me and, to the best of my knowledge, this family was shot by the Germans two days later. I was taken to another house and put in an attic and after a few hours here I saw the first doctor, Dr Merat. After seeing my hands he said I would have to be moved to the hospital to have both hands amputated to save my life.

On the way to the hospital our car was stopped by the Germans who asked to see the driver's permission to drive at night. They shone a torch into the back of the car, but as I had no clothing left to identify me as an airman they allowed us to drive on. I remember arriving at the hospital where the [Roman Catholic] sisters took charge of me. I was put on a trolley and the remnants of my battle dress were removed. I became unconscious and the next thing I remember was on the operating table[5 May]. I was asked three times for permission to amputate my hands, but by this time I was so close to being dead that I did not answer. I was given an injection in the foot and for the next two weeks I have no memory at all.

*Dr Merat arranged Bob's removal to the hospital, then located in the Hotel Dieu. The Resistance 'dumped' him at the hospital gate where the doctor 'happened' to be passing and he was quickly admitted. The Germans, who were searching for Bob, arrived a few minutes later. Had they arrived before Bob was inside the hospital gates, they would have immediately taken him for interrogation. It was revealed many years after the war that Dr Merat was a prominent member of the French Resistance, something the Germans never discovered. The doctor's report before the operation was that Bob's head was enormous because of his massive oedema, eyes inflated hiding the eyeballs, nose flattened, lips and ears burnt, and neck flattened. His hands were carbonised, comparable to those of a mummy, and gangrene was setting in. After the operation, Bob was unconscious for two weeks. His doctors tasked their daughters, Annie Merat, and 'Jenny' Lamy, with the job of nursing Bob 'around the clock', as they both spoke English* (Barbara Hunter).

The following description of events during that period is as told to me by my nurse, Jenny Daviou. My hands were placed in boxes and the necessary instruments were prepared. As the doctor was about to begin his dirty work, his wife, Madame Merat, intervened and would not allow the doctor to amputate. Dr Pierre also agreed with Madame Merat, saying that, as I was so young, I would be better off dead than without my hands.

Dr Merat then made incisions on the back and palms of my hands and along the fingers to allow the swelling to subside. I remember when regaining my senses looking at my hands and, as the bandages were so long, I knew I still had my hands. After three weeks I was told that my hands would not be amputated. They asked me foolish questions to see if my mind was working. That week the Gestapo made three attempts to interrogate me. However I made no answer [*he used the excuse that he couldn't talk because his lips were badly burnt and swollen*]. On the fourth attempt I got a little angry with it all and insulted one of the officers.

*Bob was regularly guarded by the Germans while he was in hospital, and some were a great deal more hostile than others. In one of the more amusing incidents one guard took great delight in pretending to shoot Bob. This particular intimidation ceased after the guard shot himself in the hand.*

A few days later fresh Gestapo officers came to Troyes and apparently forgot all about me. I stayed in Troyes till the Americans came [*the US Third Army arrived on 27/28 August 1944*), and after visiting all my French friends, I left for Paris. I was in Paris for five days and arrived back in England on the 13th September. I was flown back in a Douglas Dakota.

*Bob was picked up in Paris by American Military Police while sending a telegram to his parents. He was interrogated because the MPs couldn't understand his Australian accent and thought he might be a German. He was released after the senior MP saw him and identified him as an Australian.*

After the usual red tape, and much travelling around, I was given 14 days' sick leave, six of which the Air Ministry spoiled for me with interrogation. I met Stan while I was on leave; he was greatly surprised to see me alive as he was quite sure I had been killed. We spent many hours discussing what had happened and swapping experiences. I am now back in hospital for further treatment to my hands. We now know that Stan and I are the only survivors of our crew of seven. There are some things which I have not mentioned; I made arrangements with two French policemen to bring me in a civvie suit, and then assist me to escape. A few days before the Americans arrived the Germans took some of the prisoners back to Germany but left me there. That day Dr Pierre gave me an injection in the back. That same night my policemen friends came in but by this time I had a very high temperature and could not leave with them. The next morning the doctor said I had scarlet fever and had me removed to the isolation hospital, where naturally the Germans could not guard me for fear of infection. [*On 22 August the French doctor had injected Bob with the scarlet fever virus to raise his temperature and told the Germans he was infectious.*]

I was there a few days later when the battle for Troyes began. The Germans blew up a bridge beside the hospital, and the hospital roof and walls were extensively damaged. The shells were screaming overhead and we could hear them exploding nearby. The morning after the assault began I saw a body of approximately 100 Germans pass along our road, bearing rifles and light machine-guns. That day I had a very narrow escape. As I was standing out in the open a shell fragment hit my trousers and stuck in the wall behind me. I still have this as a souvenir. That day the main fighting was finished, however there were still frequent clashes and the last of the German snipers were not cleared out for four or five days. When the battle was concluded the Free French began rounding up the collaborators. Some of the men were given severe beatings, and some of them were beaten so badly that it was necessary to bring them to hospital for patching up. The women were a sight I shall never forget. When they were arrested the whole body was shaven, a Nazi swastika was painted on their front and back and then they were marched stark naked down the street to gaol. For days the city was drunk with freedom. The city was alive with members of the Free French firing their guns at mythical German snipers, and shooting each other 'in fun'—accidentally of course, but that did not prevent many of them from dying. I honestly believe that in the small portion of France which I knew, there were more of the Resistance killed accidentally than were killed in actual combat with the Germans. For instance, merely to demonstrate how trigger happy these Free French were, I was talking to the American troops on the anti-aircraft gun, which was in the park overlooked by the tower of the cathedral. Firing broke out behind us and there were about 30 Resistance men firing at the tower, they said there was a sniper there. However we did not take cover; there was one boy firing a revolver which had a barrel about 2 1/2 inches long. He was fully 200 yards from the tower, and had about has much chance of hitting the tower as I would of killing an elephant with a pea-shooter. However the park was filled with people who were only too willing to applaud his gallant effort.

When all the ammunition was finished they searched the tower and found nothing. Four times that day the tower was shot up and searched, and at night an American tank outfit came through and opened up with 50 and 70mm guns. Tracer was flying over our heads, one cut a branch from a tree overhead, we were completely demoralised when it fell and almost struck us. Some of the bullets went through the walls of the maternity ward at the hospital, the women panicked understandably, but no-one was hurt. However the American officer in charge did not see any fun in all this show of bravado, so he locked the tower and sealed the door!

*Bob Hunter met and married Barbara after his return to Australia and they had four children. Bob's injuries to his hands left him with three fingers and a thumb on each.* This made many tasks difficult but Bob adapted and there were few things he couldn't do, including playing the violin, although he was a wonderful harmonica player. Bob had studied accountancy before the war, but after the war, he preferred not to be in a 'desk job'. He studied at Gatton College and became a dairy adviser with the Queensland Department of Primary Industries.

*Bob's escape flying boots, which were removed when he was admitted to hospital, were returned to him just before he passed away in December 1972 at the age of 50. Bob's nurse, Jenny Daviou, had kept them for 28 years. Barbara Hunter passed away in September 2014.*

## Which village did Bob stumble into after the crash?

In his interview with MI5 following his return to London, Bob identified the village in which he initially sought assistance as Les Grandes-Chapelles. In a report dated 24 March 1947 and submitted to the Air Ministry in London, Flying Officer Glenn, writing on behalf of the Officer Commanding No.1 MREU, makes the following comments:

> Monsieur M.C. Drouard, Mayor of Premierfait, said he saw a burning aircraft flying overhead in the direction of Droupt-Sainte-Marie between 0030 [12.30am] and 0100 hrs[1.00am], rapidly losing altitude. Later an RAF airman came to the village and was received at his house. He had severe burns to his face and both hands. He said his Christian name was Bob. Monsieur Drouard later checked with Troyes Hospital and confirmed the airman was Bob Hunter and he was in the care of Dr Merat.

After the war Stan Jolly used maps to confirm the identity of the village he saw but passed by as Saint-Remy-sous-Barbuise, now the final resting place for both Hilton Forden and Horace Skellorn.

To place the action of the night of 4 May—Stan walking past Saint-Remy on to the village of Villacerf, Bob stumbling into Les Grandes-Chapelles, and Nan flying in the direction of Droupt-Sainte-Marie and crashing north-east of the village—requires a pretzel-shaped flight path with Colin turning for home close to the nominated point and then flying back into the path of the oncoming bombers. It would also require the Mayor of Premierfait to be living in another village.

My assessment is that Bob made his way into the village of Premierfait and the Mayor's family was not the family that offered him assistance. That particular family of four was executed in their home by the Germans.

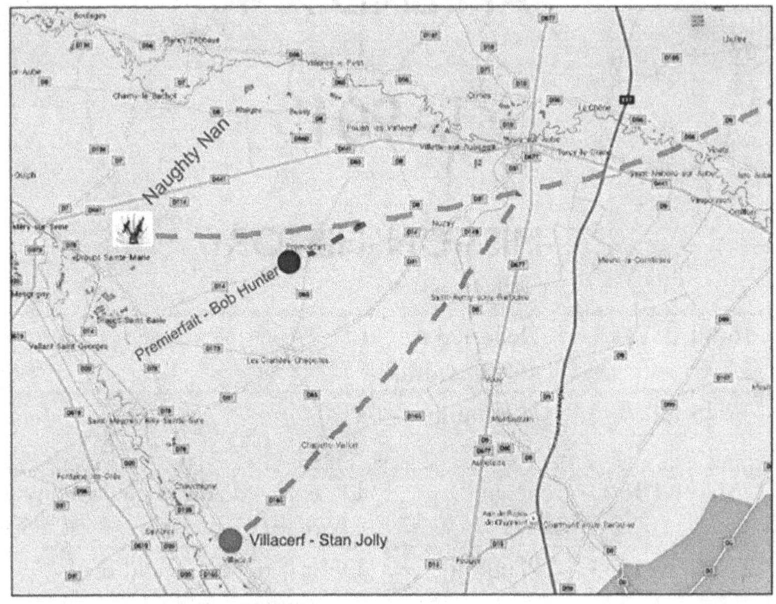


The escape routes plotted on this map are indicative, as are the points of escape from Nan. Bob Hunter and Stan Jolly both headed in a southwest direction towards Spain.

They planned to put some distance between themselves, the burning wreckage of Nan and the Germans searching for evading crewmen. Stan caught the train to Paris from Payns, just south of Villacerf (see Appendix 2) (Google map; artwork by the author).

# APPENDIX 4

# JA901

## –MISSION HISTORY

| | | | |
|---|---|---|---|
| 16 Jul 1943 | Delivered to 467 Squadron | | |
| 24/25 Jul 1943 | Hamburg | D | |
| 25/26 Jul 1943 | Essen | D | engaged and evaded enemy fighter |
| 27/28 Jul 1943 | Hamburg | D | rear turret u/s and rear gunner could not engage E/F, struggled to get to 20000 feet bombing altitude |
| 29/30 Jul 1943 | Hamburg | D | |
| 2/3 Aug 1943 | Hamburg | D | minor damage by flak |
| 7/8 Aug 1943 | Genoa | I | |
| 9/10 Aug 1943 | Mannheim | D | |
| 10/11 Aug 1943 | Nuremburg | D | |
| 12/13 Aug 1943 | Milan | I | |
| 14/15 Aug 1943 | Milan | I | ADDENDUM Major engine problems Landed Biskra, Algeria, North Africa |
| 22/23 Nov 1943 | Berlin | D | |

| | | | |
|---|---|---|---|
| 16/17 Dec 1943 | Berlin | D | Radio filled cabin with smoke and compass failure |
| 20/21 Dec 1943 | Frankfurt | D | Hydraulic failure rear turret and jettisoned bombs |
| 23/24 Dec 1943 | Berlin | D | |
| 29/30 Dec 1943 | Berlin | D | Camera failed |
| 1/2 Jan 1944 | Berlin | D | S.O. engine failure - cookie jettisoned to gain altitude |
| 2/3 Jan 1944 | Berlin | D | icing in a/c at 12500 feet - jettisoned - Landed Bardney |
| 14/15 Jan 1944 | Brunswick | D | |
| 20/21 Jan 1944 | Berlin | D | rear turret sluggish then froze up icing inside a/c at 17000 feet |
| 21/22 Jan 1944 | Magdeburg | D | |
| 27/28 Jan 1944 | Berlin | D | Landed Coleby Green |
| 28/29 Jan 1944 | Berlin | D | Pilot error, missed target, jettisoned bombs over 'Isle of Rome' |
| 30/31 Jan 1944 | Berlin | D | |
| 15/16 Feb 1944 | Berlin | D | both rear and mid-upper gunner pass out because of oxygen supply problems (other aircraft on mission have similar problem) P.O. engines lost power |
| 19/20 Feb 1944 | Leipzig | D | |
| 24/25 Feb 1944 | Schweinfurt | D | PI engine failure |
| 1/2 Mar 1944 | Stuttgart | D | Rear turret u/s before reaching target |

| | | | |
|---|---|---|---|
| 15/16 Mar 1944 | Stuttgart | D | rear turret slow and jerky and oxygen feed problems |
| 18/19 Mar 1944 | Frankfurt | D | |
| 22/23 Mar 1944 | Frankfurt | D | |
| 24/25 Mar 1944 | Berlin | D | hole in main plane from flak, landed at Metheringham |
| 10/11 Apr 1944 | Tours | F | |
| 11/12 Apr 1944 | Aachen | D | 500lb bomb failed to release - jettisoned |
| 18/19 Apr 1944 | Juvisy | F | |
| 20/21 Apr 1944 | La Chapelle | F | |
| 26/27 Apr 1944 | Schweinfurt | D | |
| 28/29 Apr 1944 | St Medards | F | SI engine fire |
| 3/4 May 1944 | Mailly | F | Failed to return |

The 467 Squadron operations sheet shows JA901 as also flown on 1/2 May 1944 on a mission to Toulouse. This is incorrect as the crew diaries record flying in ND729, PO-L.

Country codes: D – Germany, F – France, I – Italy.

# ENDNOTES

## Chapter 1

[1] Station Street has been renumbered since World War II and what was Barr & Furniss Real Estate and the Furniss residence at number 25 is now number 11.

## Chapter 2

[2] Interview with Jack Colpus, 'Australians at War' film archive, University of NSW, 2003, at: http://australiansatwarfilmarchive.unsw.edu.au/archive, accessed June 2017.

[3] Ibid.

[4] Ibid.

[5] Paul Skelly, *At the Foot of our Stairs, the History and Crews of Handley Page Halifax JD314,* self-published, US, 2011, Chapter 7.

[6] Stan Jolly, 'My Airforce Experience', unpublished memoir, 1988.

[7] Jack Colpus interview.

## Chapter 3

[8] Jack Colpus interview.

[9] Marshal of the RAF Sir Arthur Harris, *Bomber Offensive,* Pen & Sword, UK, 1947, p.97.

[10] Canadian government, 'Top Weather Events of the Twentieth Century', Environment and Climate Change Canada at: www.ec.gc.ca/meteo-weather/default.asp, accessed June 2017.

## Chapter 4

[11] Stephen Roskill, *The War at Sea, 1939–1945,* Vol. II, *The Period of Balance,* HMSO, London, 1956, p.367.

[12] Jack Colpus interview.

[13] Ibid.

[14] Leslie R. Jubbs, 'RAAF Pilots/Flight Engineer trained at RAF St Athan, 1945', self-published online, 2003 at: www.scribd.com/document/167588232/RAAF-Pilot-Engineer, accessed June 2017.

[15] Ibid.

[16] Ibid.

[17] Jolly, 'My Airforce Experience'.

[18] Bob Hunter, diary.

[19] Jolly, 'My Airforce Experience'.

[20] Flight Lieutenant Frederick Rosier, CO 229 Squadron, RAF, in Joshua Levine, *Forgotten Voices of the Blitz and the Battle for Britain,* Ebury Press, UK, 2006, p.222.

## Chapter 5

[21] Sir Arthur 'Bomber' Harris, cited in David Edgerton, *Britain's War Machine, Weapons, Resources and Experts in the Second World War,* Oxford University Press, UK, 2011, p.293.

[22] Phil Massey, 'Thank Your Lucky Stars', online article at: http://www.lancaster-archive.com, accessed June 2017.

[23] Bill Wareham, interview with Rob Marchment, 'A Piece of Cake, BBC 'World War II People's War' online interviews at: http://www.bbc.co.uk/history/ww2peopleswar/stories, accessed June 2017.

## Chapter 7

[24] John Grehan and Martin Mace, *Bomber Harris: Sir Arthur Harris' Despatches on War Operations 1942–1945,* Pen & Sword, UK, 2014, despatch 114.

[25] Flight Sergeant George Unwin, 19 Squadron, RAF, cited in Levine, *Forgotten Voices of the Blitz and the Battle for Britain,* p.189.
[26] Bob Hunter, diary.

## Chapter 8

[27] Jack Colpus interview.
[28] Bob Hunter, diary.

## Chapter 9

[29] Jack Currie, *Battle Under the Moon,* Air Data, UK, 1995.
[30] Ibid.
[31] Bob Hunter, diary.
[32] Jolly, 'My Airforce Experience'.

## Chapter 10

[33] Jolly, 'My Airforce Experience'.
[34] Bob Hunter, diary.
[35] Flight Lieutenant Frank Dixon, 467 Squadron, interview with Susan Green, Murdoch Sound Archives, Australian War Memorial.
[36] Bob Hunter, diary.
[37] Jolly, 'My Airforce Experience'.
[38] Letter from Madame Isabelle Farcy.

# Chapter 11

[39] Jack Colpus interview.

[40] Ibid.

# Chapter 13

[41] Address by M. Francois Meunier, President of the Mailly Association, 1994.

[42] David Collins, 'The Dispersal', *Dispersal,* magazine of the Newark Air Museum, August–November 2007.

# BIBLIOGRAPHY

## Books

Bowman, Martin, *Legacy of the Lancaster,* Pen & Sword Aviation, UK, 2013.

Cawthorne, Nigel, *Lancaster, WWII Night Bomber and Dambuster,* Anness Publishing Ltd, UK, 2010.

Charlwood, Don, *Journeys into Night,* Burgewood Books, Hawthorn, Victoria, 1991.

Coates, John, *Atlas of Australia's Wars,* Oxford University Press, Melbourne, 2001.

Currie, Jack, *Battle Under the Moon,* Air Data, UK, 1995.

Edgerton, David, *Britain's War Machine, Weapons, Resources and Experts in the Second World War,* Oxford University Press, UK, 2011.

Grehan, John and Mace, Martin, *Bomber Harris: Sir Arthur Harris' Despatches on War Operations 1942–1945,* Pen & Sword, UK, 2014.

Harris, Marshal of the RAF Sir Arthur, *Bomber Offensive*, Pen & Sword, UK, 1947.

Levine, Joshua, *Forgotten Voices of the Blitz and the Battle for Britain*, Ebury Press, UK, 2006.

Mennell, Gary and Mennell, Brian, *Slightly Below the Glide Path*, Vol. II, *RAF Waddington*, Fox 3 Publishing, UK, 2013.

Newark Air Museum, *Aviation in Nottinghamshire, Airfields & Memorials*, published by Newark Air Museum, UK, 2011.

Olive, Gordon and Newton, Dennis, *The Devil at 6 o'clock*, Australian Military History Publications, Loftus, NSW, 2001.

Reid, Richard, *Bomber Command – Australians in World War II*, Department of Veterans' Affairs, Canberra, 2012.

Roskill, Stephen, *The War at Sea, 1939–1945*, Vol. II, *The Period of Balance*, HMSO, London, 1956.

Skelly, Paul, *At the Foot of our Stairs, the History and Crews of Handley Page Halifax JD314*, self-published, US, 2011.

Wallace Clarke, R., *British Aircraft Armament*, Vol.1, *RAF Gun Turrets from 1914 to the Present Day*, Patrick Stephens Ltd., United Kingdom, 1993.

## Online interviews, articles and unpublished memoirs

David Collins, 'The Dispersal', *Dispersal*, magazine of the Newark Air Museum, August–November 2007.

Colpus, Jack, interview, 'Australians at War' film archive, University of NSW, 2003, at: http://australiansatwarfilmarchive.unsw.edu.au/archive.

Dixon, Flight Lieutenant Frank, 467 Squadron, RAAF, interview with Susan Green, Murdoch Sound Archives, Australian War Memorial.

Hunter, Bob, unpublished diary and account.

Jolly, Stan, 'My Airforce Experience', unpublished memoir, 1988.

Jubbs, Leslie R., 'RAAF Pilots/Flight Engineer trained at RAF St Athan, 1945', self-published online, 2003 at: www.scribd.com/document/167588232/RAAF-Pilot-Engineer.

Massey, Phil, 'Thank Your Lucky Stars', online article at: http://www.lancasterarchive.com, accessed June 2017.

Wareham, Bill, interview with Rob Marchment, 'A Piece of Cake', BBC 'World War II People's War' online interviews at: http://www.bbc.co.uk/history/ww2peopleswar/stories.

***Available now online or at all good bookstores***

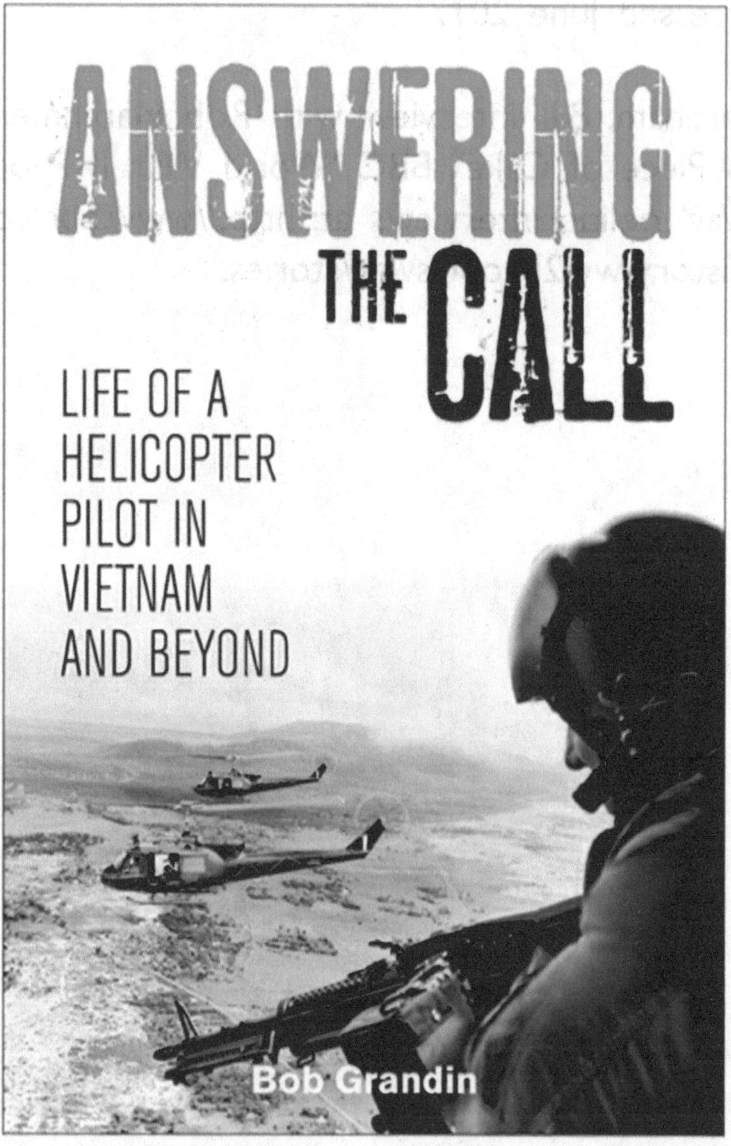


View sample pages, reviews and more information on this and other titles at www.bigskypublishing.com.au

# BACK COVER MATERIAL

BIG SKY PUBLISHING

*Brief Mission* is the story of Australian navigator Oscar Dumas just one of [illegible] young men who perished while flying for Bomber Command during World War II. Lovingly crafted by his nephew Mal Elliott, this book brings to life a young man whose name was never spoken by his family and who was a stranger to his modern-day descendants.

Elliott follows Oscar from his carefree childhood in the Blue Mountains, through his training over the vast emptiness of Canada, to the mysterious patchwork landscape of Britain and on to the hostile skies of occupied France. He uses the accounts of the two surviving aircrew to piece together the events of the fateful night that saw most of the crew of Lancaster [illegible], affectionately known as Naughty Nan, of which its pilot Colin Dickson heroically manoeuvred his burning aircraft away from the towns and villages that dotted the landscape. This has been a difficult book for Elliott to write as it contains a harrowing description of his uncle's last moments. The terrible moments of the deaths of the aircrew are vividly described alongside the miraculous tales of the two survivors.

# BACK COVER MATERIAL

*Fatal Mission* is the story of Australian navigator Oscar Furniss, just one of 55,000 young men who perished while flying for Bomber Command during World War II. Lovingly crafted by his nephew, Mal Elliott, this book brings to life a young man whose name was never spoken by his family and who was a stranger to his modern-day descendants.

Elliott follows Oscar from his carefree childhood in the Blue Mountains through his training over the vast emptiness of Canada to the mist-shrouded patchwork landscapes of Britain and on to the hostile skies of occupied France. He uses the accounts of the two surviving aircrew to piece together the events of the fateful night that saw most of the crew of Lancaster JA901, a fractionally know as Naughty Nan, perish as pilot Colin Dickson heroically manoeuvred his burning aircraft away from the towns and villages that dotted the landscape. This has been a difficult book for Elliott to write as it contains a harrowing description of his uncle's last moments. The terrible impact of the deaths of the aircrew are vividly described alongside the miraculous tales of the two survivors.

But for the family of Oscar Furniss there would be no miracle, just the lingering weight of deep and lasting grief. This is a story that moves beyond the technical descriptions of bombing missions to describe the human toll of conflict. It underlines the crucial importance of commemoration, of refusing to allow those who perished in war to be forgotten. Theirs was a sacrifice that we who live in freedom should never forget.

www.ingramcontent.com/pod-product-compliance
Lightning Source LLC
Chambersburg PA
CBHW010717300426
44114CB00022B/2886

* 9 7 8 0 3 6 9 3 9 1 2 0 9 *